101 MOST POWERFUL PROMISES IN THE BIBLE

101
MOST
POWERFUL
PROMISES
IN THE
BIBLE

Steve and Lois Rabey

General Editors
and

Marcia Ford

WARNER
Faith

A Division of AOL Time Warner Book Group

Published in association with the literary agency of Alive Communications, Inc., 7680 Goddard Street, Suite 200, Colorado Springs, CO 80920.

Unless otherwise noted, Scripture quotations are from the HOLY BIBLE: NEW INTERNATIONAL VERSION®. Copyright © 1973, 1978, 1984 by International Bible Society. Used by permission of Zondervan Bible Publishers. All rights reserved.

Scripture quotations noted NKJV are from the NEW KING JAMES VERSION. Copyright © 1979, 1980, 1982, Thomas Nelson, Inc., Publishers.

Scripture quotations noted AMP are from THE AMPLIFIED BIBLE: Old Testament. Copyright © 1962, 1964 by Zondervan Publishing House (used by permission); and from THE AMPLIFIED NEW TESTAMENT. Copyright © 1958 by the Lockman Foundation (used by permission).

Scripture quotations noted NASB are from the NEW AMERICAN STANDARD BIBLE®. © Copyright The Lockman Foundation 1960, 1962, 1963, 1968, 1971, 1972, 1973, 1975, 1977. Used by permission.

Warner Books, Inc., 1271 Avenue of the Americas, New York, NY 10020.

Visit our website at www.twbookmark.com

WARNER *Faith*™ A Division of AOL Time Warner Book Group

Printed in the United States of America

First Warner Books printing: October 2003

10 9 8 7 6 5 4 3 2 1

ISBN: 0-446-53214-2
LCCN: 2003106450

To John, Elizabeth, and Sarah

Acknowledgments

My thanks first and foremost go to Chip MacGregor at Alive Communications for giving me the opportunity to take on this project. I also wish to acknowledge the fact that Steve Rabey resisted whatever temptation he might have experienced to get even with me, since I once edited *his* work. Instead, he graciously suggested several ideas that improved the book, and he and Lois capably ushered the manuscript through the initial editing process.

As always, I need to thank my longsuffering family, especially a daughter who once asked me in exasperation, "Are you ever going to get one of those income jobs?" Working from home does have a drawback or two. I love having my family nearby as I'm writing, though I can't say they feel the same way. Still, they take good care of me, if only out of pity.

Contents

General Editors' Preface   xiii
Introduction   xv

1. Unbridled Joy   1
2. Wisdom from Above   4
3. Prosperous Plans   7
4. Rest for Your Soul   10
5. A Way Out   13
6. Abiding in the Vine   15
7. Jumping through Religious Hoops   18
8. Divine Guidance   20
9. A Three-Pronged Promise   23
10. A Garment of Praise   26
11. This Is the Way   28
12. Life Everlasting   31
13. Fearless Fighter   33
14. Unmerited Favor   35
15. My Father's House   37
16. "I Have Called You Friends"   40
17. Overtaken by Blessing   42
18. Watch Him Flee   45
19. A Good Measure   47
20. Mountain-Moving Faith   49

21. Do What?　　　　　　　　　　　51
22. Godly Character　　　　　　　　53
23. Loving the Unlovable　　　　　　55
24. Total Renovation　　　　　　　　57
25. Enjoying God　　　　　　　　　59
26. Sounds in the Night　　　　　　61
27. Case Dismissed　　　　　　　　63
28. No Expiration Date　　　　　　66
29. Repairing a Broken Heart　　　68
30. A Wholehearted Pursuit　　　　70
31. True Confession　　　　　　　　72
32. Delighting in the Word　　　　75
33. "What Is Truth?"　　　　　　　78
34. Working for the Good　　　　　80
35. Healing the Land　　　　　　　83
36. Rest from Labor　　　　　　　　85
37. Prophets of Integrity　　　　　87
38. Infinite Patience　　　　　　　90
39. Supernatural Strength　　　　　92
40. Muttering Your Meditation　　94
41. Already Clean　　　　　　　　　96
42. Comfort for the Afflicted　　　98
43. Full to Overflowing　　　　　101
44. He Will Do What He Says　　103
45. The Lord Will Provide　　　　105
46. Supernatural Teacher　　　　　108
47. Eternal Trophy　　　　　　　　110
48. A "More Full" Life　　　　　　113
49. The Spoils of War　　　　　　115
50. Deliverance from Trouble　　117
51. Glory after Death　　　　　　119

52. A God Who Hears   121
53. Great Is His Faithfulness   123
54. The Water and the Fire   126
55. God's Justice   129
56. Avenging Wrong   131
57. Invited Guest   134
58. Bond of Love   136
59. A Lasting Covenant   138
60. Wordless Prayer   141
61. A Forgetting God   143
62. Emissaries from God   145
63. The Way They Should Go   148
64. An Astonishing Act   150
65. A Sentry over Your Heart and Mind   152
66. The Power of Persistent Prayer   155
67. We Shall Be Like Him   158
68. A New Baptism   160
69. Security in an Insecure World   162
70. Never Give Up   164
71. Humbling Yourself   166
72. Have Fun—and Be Holy   168
73. Your Part in an Eternal Drama   170
74. A Divine Inheritance   173
75. A Permanent Register   175
76. Getting to Know God   177
77. May It Go Well with You   179
78. No Condemnation   181
79. Simple Obedience   183
80. Forbidden Territory   185
81. Anxiety-Free Living   187
82. Your Place in Heaven   189

83. A Profound Peace 191

84. Prayer Offered in Faith 193

85. Power for Service 196

86. Strength in Numbers 198

87. Purpose of God's Word 200

88. Strength for the Journey 202

89. To Be Young Again 205

90. Sharing in Christ's Resurrection 208

91. Praise from God 210

92. Safe from Evil 212

93. Salvation of Your Family 214

94. The Second Coming of Christ 216

95. Sleeping in Heavenly Peace 218

96. Authority over the Enemy 220

97. The Body and the Blood 222

98. Let There Be Light 224

99. Even Greater Things 226

100. The Breath of the Almighty 228

101. Unified but Not Uniform 231

Notes 233

General Editors' Preface

There are thousands of verses in the Bible. How can we find the ones containing the divine wisdom and guidance we are looking for, in order to help us grow spiritually and live more faithfully? This book and others in the 101 Most Powerful series will help you find and unlock powerful passages of Scripture that inspire, comfort, and challenge.

101 Most Powerful Prayers in the Bible helps us open our hearts to God by showing us how earlier saints and sinners prayed.

101 Most Powerful Promises in the Bible brings together those passages that convey God's boundless and eternal love for his creation and his creatures.

101 Most Powerful Proverbs in the Bible will enable us to apply God's timeless truths to many of the messy details of daily life.

And *101 Most Powerful Verses in the Bible* provides a treasury of divine insight gathered from nearly every book of the Old and New Testaments.

You're probably familiar with Marcia Ford, the author of this volume, who has written a dozen books and edited many others. A journalist at heart, she has also worked as an editor for a major newspaper, a website, and several Christian magazines.

As you'll see for yourself as soon as you dive into the following pages, Marcia has a thorough knowledge of the Bible and an ability to explain God's promises in a way that is both informative and accessible. If you're seeking encouragement or a reminder of God's ongoing work in your life, you'll find both here, thanks to her hard work and warm style.

This and the other books in this series will never replace the Bible, but we do hope they will help you grasp its powerful and life-changing lessons and better utilize its wisdom in your life.

Steve and Lois Rabey

Introduction

God is not a man, that he should lie,
nor a son of man, that he should change his mind.
Does he speak and then not act?
Does he promise and not fulfill?

Numbers 23:19

Thank God! Thank him that he is not a man, that he does not lie or change his mind. Unlike our flesh-and-blood friends—unlike ourselves—God does not break his promises. Nor does he make them lightly. No, when God says he's going to do something, you can count on him to make good on it. The Creator of the universe does exactly what he says he is going to do.

And he says it frequently, underscoring our need to be told over and over again that he means what he says. Still, we live in utter disbelief that he could possibly love us as much as his promises imply. So he scatters them abundantly throughout the Bible, knowing we need the constant reassurance that he is not like our promise-breaking friends—not like ourselves.

Some of those promises, of course, he made to specific people at specific times, such as this one to Joshua: "No one will be able to stand up against you all the days of your life. As I was with Moses, so I will be with you; I will never leave you nor forsake you" (Josh.

1:5). But as a man of unwavering faith in God, Joshua represents faithful believers; the underlying principle of God's promise to Joshua applies to all his faithful followers.

The fact is, we can't read his Word for very long without coming across yet another ironclad guarantee from the Father. *101 Most Powerful Promises in the Bible* pulls many of those guarantees together for you. Do you need to believe God can heal you physically? That he can help you overcome depression or resist temptation? That he will answer your prayers and give you guidance? You don't have to wait until you happen to come across those assurances in your daily reading. Just turn to the devotional in this book that addresses your immediate need. You'll find a Bible verse that expresses a promise God has made regarding that need, some thoughts on how you can apply that promise to your life today, a suggested prayer, and references pointing to additional verses that pertain to your situation. You might also consider reading the devotionals in a systematic way, so you'll be familiar with the key promises God has made to you in his Word. After all, you can't claim his promises if you don't know what they are.

Once you become familiar with the scriptural guarantees, you need to follow up by believing the foundational promise that God will in fact do what he says he will do. In laying hold of that truth, you exhibit the kind of faith that God says is necessary to inherit all of his assurances (Heb. 6:11–12). When you begin to inherit his promises—when you start living as if he means what he says—you will experience his love to a depth and a degree you never thought possible. And you will finally be able to exchange your utter disbelief for the inexpressible security of his love.

101
MOST
POWERFUL
PROMISES
IN THE
BIBLE

1

Unbridled Joy

*He will yet fill your mouth with laughter
and your lips with shouts of joy.*

Job 8:21

HAVE you ever felt as if someone passed you by when handing out the gift of joy? Sometimes you're simply mired in a joy-less disposition. You slog through days or weeks when you just can't seem to surface from a serious funk. You know the Bible tells you to be joyful, but when you're down in the dumps, verses such as Philippians 4:4 (NKJV)—"Rejoice in the Lord always. Again I will say, rejoice!"—fall on your deaf ears.

Those are the kinds of verses your friends are most likely to quote in a well-meaning but futile attempt to cheer you up. It's all well and good for others to tell you to rejoice, but just once, wouldn't it be great if someone would tell you how?

Fortunately, God not only *wants* you to rejoice in him, but he also promises to *enable* you to rejoice in him. Jesus—who, by the way, cannot be separated from joy—said God will give you the kind of joy that no one can ever take away from you (John 16:22). And just look at the way God makes that promise throughout the Bible. Some verses use such vivid imagery that it's clear he's talking about a wild and holy and unbridled joy: you'll dance your way out of sorrow and sadness (Jer. 31:13) as the mountains and hills break into song, to the hand-clapping beat of the trees strutting their stuff in the fields (Isa. 55:12). If nothing else, it would be worth climbing out of the pit just to catch a glimpse of that picture.

God knows when and why you're feeling low, and he doesn't want you to compound your misery with guilty feelings because you can't perk up the way everyone seems to think you should. Instead, he wants to place within you the kind of joy that circumstances can never touch, the kind that flows from an intimate relationship with him. But you have to open your heart to him and believe he will restore the joy of your salvation (Ps. 51:12), just as David asked him to. Take a step of faith by reading out loud the Scripture verses that promise joy, like these:

- You have made known to me the path of life; you will fill me with joy in your presence, with eternal pleasures at your right hand. (Psalm 16:11)

- The precepts of the LORD are right, giving joy to the heart. The commands of the LORD are radiant, giving light to the eyes. (Psalm 19:8)

- When anxiety was great within me, your consolation brought joy to my soul. (Psalm 94:19)

- Those who sow in tears will reap with songs of joy. (Psalm 126:5)

- I have told you this so that my joy may be in you and that your joy may be complete. (John 15:11)

As you read, your words will become a prayer to God.

Once you've broken the barrier that keeps you from experiencing genuine joy, your capacity for delight will begin to expand—and you'll start to wonder how you can possibly contain it all. You can't, which is exactly what God intended. You'll find yourself giving away the excess, and the overflow will prove irresistible to those around you. Not bad for someone who just yesterday, it seems, couldn't even "Rejoice!"

———

Lord, I ask for the grace to trust you to restore to me the kind of joy no one can take away and no circumstance can touch. I thank you for the unbridled, overflowing joy that comes from knowing you.

2

Wisdom from Above

If any of you lacks wisdom, he should ask God, who gives generously to all without finding fault, and it will be given to him.

James 1:5

THIS is one promise that packs such a powerful punch, it could change the course of your life. If you think that's an overstatement, consider this: there are only two ways to acquire wisdom—through your experiences and through the counsel of others. If you rely on yourself, you're looking at years, maybe decades, of trial and error to figure out how to live this one life you've been given. You'll go through trials, and you'll have to live with the consequences of the errors in judgment you make. Clearly, this would not be the preferred way to acquire wisdom, though it seems to be the most widely followed.

If you rely on the counsel of others, you still have one more choice to make. Will you trust the wisdom that comes from the culture around you—or the kind that comes from above, from God himself? Without realizing it, many of us fall victim to earthly wisdom. We hear advice that sounds reasonable; without comparing it to the time-tested Word of God, we go ahead and follow it. In an age replete with self-help books, Internet chat rooms, and psychological studies on everything under the sun, it's difficult to avoid the wisdom of the world.

That's why God's promise to grant you wisdom is so powerful. You can know, with absolute certainty, that the way you've chosen to live and think and react is based on God's divine guidance. Seismic cultural shifts register a big fat zero on your version of the Richter scale; the ground beneath your feet remains firm and unmoving, because the Creator of the universe has led you to solid ground—the wisdom he established long before you made your appearance on earth. And as with the other promises he makes in the Bible, God does not equivocate on this. He states it flat out: he *will* give you wisdom; all you have to do is ask.

That's all Solomon did, and he was considered the wisest man alive during his time (1 Kings 4:29–31). Look at what God said to him:

> Since this is your heart's desire and you have not asked for wealth, riches or honor . . . but for wisdom and knowledge to govern my people over whom I have made you king, therefore wisdom and knowledge will be given you. And I will also give you wealth, riches and honor, such as no king who was before you ever had and none after you will have. (2 Chron. 1:11–12)

Wisdom from above changed the course of Solomon's life. Let it change yours as well, by trusting God to make good on his promise.

Lord, help me desire your wisdom above everything the world has to offer. Give me a heart for wanting to do things your way, regardless of how different your way may appear to others.

3

Prosperous Plans

"For I know the plans I have for you," declares the LORD, "plans to prosper you and not to harm you, plans to give you hope and a future."

Jeremiah 29:11

SITTING at the bottom of a deep pit in the valley of Shechem as others decided his fate, Joseph must have had second thoughts about the grand and glorious future the Lord seemed to have promised him through his dreams. His brothers had plotted to kill him; he must have been bewildered when they reached down to pull him out after they seemingly had left him to die.

Deliverance! he may have thought. But no, his brothers handed him over to a band of Egyptians who needed another slave. Over the years, as he worked his way up in the household of Potiphar, Joseph must have thought he finally had it made. Instead, one false accusation landed him in jail, betrayed and forgotten. It didn't look as if God's plan for him included prosperity or hope or even a future.

Eventually, the right person remembered Joseph and his ability to correctly interpret dreams. At the time, Pharaoh desperately needed a correct interpretation for one of his dreams: in it, seven emaciated cows devoured seven fat cows and seven puny ears of corn devoured seven fat ears of corn. Joseph explained that the dream meant that seven years of famine would follow seven years of plenty, and that Pharaoh needed to prepare for those lean years during the coming prosperous years.

Impressed by Joseph's acumen, Pharaoh elevated him to a position of tremendous power as an administrator second only to Pharaoh himself. In this position, Joseph became a blessing not only to the people of Egypt but also to his own long-lost family, who were to suffer the effects of the famine back in Egypt. Forced to go to Pharaoh for help, Joseph's brothers were brought before Joseph to request grain from Egypt's vast storehouses; they did not recognize the brother they had betrayed, but he recognized them. But instead of retaliating against them, Joseph eventually reunited the entire family and even provided a home for them in Goshen, where they would be closer to him and the abundant food that Joseph had wisely stockpiled.

Whenever you need a solid dose of hope regarding God's plans for your future, read about Joseph's little Egyptian adventure in Genesis 37–47. You'd be hard-pressed to find a more powerful example of God coming through on his promises amid unlikely circumstances. Despite decades of testing, Joseph waited in patient expectation for the promises of God to be fulfilled.

Even so, the Bible tells us that "God had planned something better for us" (Heb. 11:40), better than the fulfillment of his promises to Joseph—because unlike Joseph, we know the Messiah. What's more, God has given the Holy Spirit to indwell and guide us. That's a blessing we can hardly fathom.

We do manage to complicate and misinterpret that blessing, though. A fellow believer may warn you that you should never take a single step until you have unmistakable guidance from the Lord.

That suggests you should wait for divine direction before you get out of bed in the morning. You have known other people who make elaborate plans for their lives, say a quick prayer asking God to bless their plans, and mentally slap the Holy Spirit Seal of Approval on what they have already decided to do.

God does not want you living at either extreme. He has given you freedom to live the abundant life, not one that keeps you chained to your bed for fear of a single misstep. And he's given the Holy Spirit to empower you to walk in the assurance that the Lord is indeed directing your steps. He simply wants you to commit your way to him; he promises that his plans will prosper you by giving you hope and a future.

———————

Lord, I hand over to you those plans for my life that I made without your guidance; do with them whatever you will. I thank you for sending the Holy Spirit to guide me as I seek, and attempt to live out, your will for my life.

4

Rest for Your Soul

Come to me, all you who are weary and burdened, and I will give you rest. Take my yoke upon you and learn from me, for I am gentle and humble in heart, and you will find rest for your souls.

Matthew 11:28–29

R EST? What's that? In our culture, the notion of setting aside time to do nothing is practically laughable. In church, we nod in agreement as we're told that we should be more like Mary, who sat at Jesus' feet and learned from him, and less like Martha, who fussed and fumed and worked her way into a self-righteous snit. And then we go right back to the task-driven, exhausting lifestyle of a modern-day Martha.

Meanwhile, lying between the covers of our Bibles are numerous verses that encourage us to "come aside" and leave the busyness of our daily routines for a while. "Come away by yourselves to a de-serted place, and rest a while," Jesus said to his disciples in Mark 6:31 (AMP). The constant presence of the crowds that Jesus attracted was taking a toll on his followers, and "they had not even leisure enough to eat." Surely they knew the words of the prophets; it was through Isaiah that God reminded the Israelites, "In repentance and rest you will be saved, in quietness and trust is your strength" (Isa. 30:15 NASB). Through the prophet Jeremiah, he gave this advice to his people: "Stand by the ways and see and ask for the ancient paths, where the good way is, and walk in it; and you will find rest for your souls" (Jer. 6:16 NASB).

When God tells you, "I will give you rest" (Exod. 33:14), he means it. God doesn't engage in religious-sounding talk. When he speaks, you can believe what he says. But you can't very well ask God to give you rest as you continue to scurry about, your mind and body still engaged in never-ending activity.

Take advantage of this promise of God. Set aside time to stop your normal routine. Ask God to enable you to clear your mind and learn to abide in him; ask him to help you believe that his promise of rest is still valid in the twenty-first century.

Enlist the support of your family and friends by explaining to them that from now on you will be taking personal time when you prefer not to be disturbed unless there's an emergency. Find a place where you can be alone—a room in your house or a nearby park or a quiet corner in a library or bookstore.

Spend time reading the Bible or another inspirational book, out of love for God and not out of a sense of duty. Spend time in prayer, writing out your prayers if you're in a public place. And spend time doing nothing at all, just listening to the thoughts in your mind and getting to know yourself all over again.

In recent years, many believers have returned to a more contemplative way of life. They've said "Enough!" to the whirlwind of commotion that threatened to engulf them, and they've learned to carve out spaces in their days when they leave the bustle behind and enter into the rest God promises. You may not be drawn to that lifestyle, but you can draw inspiration from it, knowing that others—maybe even some of your own neighbors or coworkers—are closing the door on the world's perpetual motion and finding quietness for their souls throughout the day.

It is possible. And even better, it is promised—by the one who never makes a promise he doesn't keep.

———————

Lord, you know I need a break—and you know how I've failed in my efforts to take that break. Lord, I believe you will give me perfect rest as you promised. Teach me how to relax in your presence.

5

A Way Out

No temptation has seized you except what is common to man. And God is faithful; he will not let you be tempted beyond what you can bear. But when you are tempted, he will also provide a way out so that you can stand up under it.

1 Corinthians 10:13

Y OU'RE pitching a product to a client, and before you know it, you're exaggerating its features. To celebrate the sale, you ignore your doctor's warnings and drop by Starbucks for a latté and Rocky Road truffles. As you wait in line, you recognize a familiar voice, edge closer, and eavesdrop on two colleagues talking about a company vice president who just got the boot.

No doubt about it—those temptations are common to man and woman. An exaggeration, a dietary infraction, a bit of gossip: we hardly pay attention to the many temptations we fail to resist in a single day. But on days when our spiritual senses are sharper than usual, our conscience will not let us rest.

Still, we go through a mental gymnastics routine that would put an Olympic athlete to shame: *Well, she'll be happy with our product, even without the features I described. This is only my second bag of truffles this week, and I wasn't the one gossiping. I was an innocent bystander.*

This would be a good time to stop the gymnastics routine. Look back over your day and ask God to show you the opportunities you had to resist the many temptations you faced. Don't just look at your failures, though—pay attention to the many victories you experienced as well. Can you see the bright red *Exit* signs he flashed before you? How many did you follow? God's Word promises that he will provide a "way out," a means of escaping temptation. His escape routes often come in the form of your conscience, warning you to stop—*now*—before you engage in any activity that you know is wrong, including any activity that you know is wrong *for you.*

Maybe you're wrestling with a much deeper issue, an addictive sin that seems to have a stranglehold on you. If you are involved in an adulterous relationship, or you can't seem to overcome your attraction to pornography, or you suffer from chronic depression, you are not alone. If that's the case, though, you may need professional counseling, which can help bring you out of the deep darkness. From there, God can lead you safely through the shadows to the *Exit* sign he has posted for you, the one that will take you from the darkness of sin to the light of his forgiveness.

Remember this: when Jesus faced temptation, he found the perfect way out—the Word of God. As Jesus repeated the words God had spoken, the tempter realized he didn't stand a chance. No matter what temptation you are facing today, the Word of God has the power to utterly demolish it.

———

Lord, I confess the trouble I have resisting temptation. I ask you to remind me to look always for the way out the instant I'm tempted to do wrong.

6

Abiding in the Vine

I am the vine; you are the branches. If a man remains in me and I in him, he will bear much fruit; apart from me you can do nothing.

John 15:5

ARE you the kind of person who wants—no, *needs*—to see results? To you, the most satisfying days are those that end with some evidence of your labor: a hefty amount of cash in the register; a certain number of deals clinched; every room in the house sparkling clean—all at the same time, no less. The most frustrating days are those that close with loose ends lying around all over the place, despite your hard work.

Most frustrating of all for you as a believer is not seeing any fruit from your spiritual labor. Granted, much of the fruit Christians bear is not evident, or at least not immediately so. You may never know how your kindness, your prayers, or your evangelistic efforts have impacted another person's life. But still . . . you know that you should be able to see *some* fruitfulness in your life as a believer. So why don't you?

The key may be found in the promise Jesus made in John 15:5.

He starts out with the metaphor of a living plant, a vine. He said he is the vine itself, the strong supporting "trunk" through which water and nutrients flow. Believers are the branches that draw their nourishment, their very lives, from the vine. Those branches that produce fruit are the ones that have clung to the vine—to Jesus, relying on him for their sustenance. Those that fail to produce fruit are those that try to do it on their own, with dismal results.

Your fruitfulness depends on your faithfulness in drawing on all that Jesus has to offer, and that requires "remaining" in him. The word for "remaining" can also be translated as "abiding"—dwelling in him, resting in him, counting on him to continue to provide all you need for spiritual fruitfulness. Are you truly abiding in him? If so, you can be sure you will bear much fruit. If not, well, you can be sure your efforts will fail in the eyes of God. Abiding in Christ means living in such a close relationship with him that your spirit is in tune with his. You become conformed to the image of Christ (Rom. 8:29), and you are transformed as your mind becomes renewed (Rom. 12:2). How can you know you are abiding in Christ? Your obedience to him, an act that springs from your love for him, is the key.

Lots of well-meaning Christians expend enormous amounts of energy engaged in pointless religious activity. They *think* they know what they should be doing to usher in the kingdom of God, but they've reached their conclusions apart from an abiding, living dependence on Jesus. The more they spin their religious wheels, the less they accomplish.

Don't be numbered among them. Relax. Learn to abide in him. See yourself as one of those metaphorical branches, a believer who knows your sustenance comes from the vine. You'll be bearing fruit in no time—both the kind you can see and the greater crop that you can't see.

———

Lord, teach me what it means to truly abide in you. Keep reminding me that my fruitfulness depends on my ability to remain in you and not on my own efforts. I rejoice in the results I can see, and I trust you that there are more that I cannot see.

7

Jumping through Religious Hoops

If we confess our sins, he is faithful and just and will forgive us our sins and purify us from all unrighteousness.

1 John 1:9

I n centuries past, and even today in some cultures and religious traditions, many among the faithful have believed that they must perform some severe penitential act as a means of earning God's forgiveness. Shrines throughout the world bear witness to this misguided thinking, and not just in undeveloped areas; even today, at a place like St. Joseph's Oratory in the very cosmopolitan city of Montreal, you can see pilgrims on hands and knees, crawling up the hundred or so steps that lead to the shrine, all in an effort to please God and gain his forgiveness so he will heal them.

But God offers forgiveness freely in response to only one penitential act, the act of confession. So what is it that causes us to complicate the most simple truths? Perhaps our guilt is so great that we cannot accept the simplicity of spiritual truths such as God's pardon. So we add all kinds of conditions to his promise and create a succession of religious hoops we feel we must jump through in order to receive mercy. In truth, we take those actions to *feel* forgiven. *Being* forgiven is another matter entirely.

The process of *being* forgiven starts when you agree with God about sin, both in general and specific terms, which is what confession is all about. You acknowledge your overall sinfulness and the particular sins you have committed, but your acknowledgment goes far beyond an intellectual understanding. A deep sorrow in your spirit, an awareness that your sin has grieved God and broken off your communion with him, evidences genuine confession.

The beauty of the promise in 1 John 1:9 lies in the restoration of that communion. When you confess your sin in the spirit of true repentance, you also make a decision to turn from that sin, because you know that to continue in it would mean a prolonged break in your fellowship with God. Real confession, then, involves not only agreeing with God about your sin but also refusing to indulge in that sin anymore. If you *genuinely* confess your sin, he promises to forgive and purify you. You can *know* you are forgiven.

Does this verse mean that if you fail to confess each and every sin in your life, he will not forgive you? No—because no one can ever accomplish that, though there are some believers who think otherwise, despite the fact that our sinful thoughts alone could make confession a twenty-four-hour-a-day activity. Don't allow yourself to get hung up on details that can distract you from a larger, more significant truth. Confess the sins that the Holy Spirit reveals to you, accept God's forgiveness, and get on with the life he wants you to lead.

———

Lord, I thank you for the forgiveness you so freely give. Help me to see the simplicity of your truth—and keep me from creating obstacles to experiencing your peace.

8

Divine Guidance

I will instruct you and teach you in the way you should go;
I will counsel you and watch over you.

Psalm 32:8

So many choices, so little time. Isn't that the way life feels some-times? We're blessed with an abundance of opportunity, and we have little reason to complain. But of course, we do. We want to do it all, see it all, experience it all—and yet we can't, if for no other reason than the fact that we're locked in to this thing called time.

And time is something we don't want to waste. We dread the thought of spending years in a dead-end job, an unfulfilling marriage, or an area of the country that we hate. Our every choice is important, because each one leads to another. Meanwhile, we're trying to live our lives to the fullest. How can we possibly be sure that we get the most out of them?

Psalm 32:8 offers a clue. In this verse, God promises to lead us in the way we should go, watching over us and guiding along the way. But for him to do this, we must be alert and attentive to his leading. We need to keep our eyes on him and keep our ears tuned in to the sound of his voice—that still, small voice that speaks to our spirit, always instructing us, always teaching us, always guiding us. Most of all, we need to trust that he will not lead us astray.

The Old Testament Book of Ruth offers a great illustration of what happened in the life of one woman who trusted God so completely that she made the choice to leave her people—everything that was familiar to her—and venture into an unknown land with her mother-in-law, Naomi. She humbled herself by working as a gleaner in the fields of Boaz. By allowing God—a God she hardly knew at first—to direct her steps, she found love, marriage, and a fulfilling life that she could not have imagined on the day she left Moab and set out for Bethlehem with Naomi.

Ruth lived in a time and a place that offered very few choices for a young widow. The one she made was by far the riskiest, but to her, the choice was clear, and she believed Naomi's God would be with her every step of the way.

By contrast, your choices are plentiful—and God promises to be with you every step of the way as well. Don't allow an abundance of opportunity to become a source of confusion in your life. Lay your choices before God. Take advantage of all the resources available to you for discerning his will. Pray about the decisions you need to make, asking God to guide you toward the right choice. Discover the biblical principles that apply to your situation; an online searchable Bible or a topical Bible can help immensely. Seek out the counsel of Christians you admire and respect. List the pros and cons for each of the choices you have. Then bring it all before God once again and allow him the opportunity to give you peace about the direction in which you should go.

———

Lord, thank you for the many choices you have given me. I place them before you in confidence, knowing that you will guide me in the way I should go.

9

A Three-Pronged Promise

No one will be able to stand up against you all the days of your life. As I was with Moses, so I will be with you; I will never leave you nor forsake you.

Joshua 1:5

At first glance, this verse appears simply to promise that God's presence will always be with you. And it does that, but it guarantees much more as well. Embedded in this one verse of Scripture are three promises: victory over enemies, an intimate relationship with God, and God's everlasting presence.

"No one will be able to stand up against you." In making this promise to Joshua, God was ensuring his victory over the many enemies he and the Israelites would face in the new land God had given to them. The principle behind the promise carries over to your life as well: as you walk in the ways of God, as Joshua did, you can be assured that no enemy—no undermining coworker, no rebellious child, no abusive spouse, no betraying friend—will be able to claim victory over you. No attacker will have the ability to stand up against you when you are in the presence of the Lord.

Maybe it doesn't look that way to you right now. Your enemy seems to have the upper hand. He clearly intends to win this fight, no matter what it takes. But what he doesn't realize is that he is powerless to hurt you when God's invisible shield of protection surrounds you. It may look for all the world like he's getting to you. God's grace, though, is much tougher than it sounds. Draw on that grace and stand on God's promise to be with you.

"As I was with Moses, so I will be with you." Like Joshua, you can have the same kind of relationship with the Lord that Moses had. What kind was that? It was a personal, one-on-one relationship. You can approach the holy Creator of the universe knowing that he will receive you as he would a friend, and you can share your life with him on a profoundly deep level.

"I will never leave you nor forsake you." Joshua was about to lead a stubborn group of people out of their forty-year sojourn in the wilderness and into the land God promised them—a land inhabited by idol-worshipers and belligerent nations. God's presence was absolutely necessary if Joshua was to succeed. By using both terms— "leave" and "forsake"—God is saying the same thing twice, no doubt because he realized how many times his people needed—and still need—to hear something in order to believe it. Regardless of how you feel, no matter how far away the Lord may seem, he is always with you. Even in your darkest days and nights, even in your spiritually dry times, even in your times of rebellion, he is there.

These words empowered Joshua as he dared to continue his journey with the recalcitrant Israelites. They can empower you, too, as you continue your faith journey with the Lord.

———

Lord, you have said that no one will be able to stand up against me; remind me of that when my enemies besiege me. You have welcomed me as a friend; bring that to my mind when I feel unworthy to come to you. You have promised never to leave me; let me never forget that, even when you seem nowhere to be found.

10

A Garment of Praise

[He has sent me] to provide for those who grieve in Zion—
to bestow on them a crown of beauty instead of ashes,
the oil of gladness instead of mourning,
and a garment of praise instead of a spirit of despair.
They will be called oaks of righteousness,
a planting of the LORD for the display of his splendor.

Isaiah 61:3

How can a Christian—one who has been born into a new life in Christ, an abundant life of blessing beyond measure—ever sink into a spirit of despair? Easily. In fact, all too easily.

By nature, Christians have high expectations of both God and themselves. But they also have a painful awareness of their own shortcomings and sinfulness. Furthermore, they're maligned, misunderstood, and persecuted, and they have a hard time giving themselves permission to vent their anger about all that. It's no wonder they—or rather, we—frequently fall victim to serious cases of depression.

Depression sometimes is anger turned inward, and that makes us as believers especially vulnerable to its devastating effects. We get mad at God because he seems to have forgotten us or to have failed to come through for us, and we mistakenly believe that it's wrong to express our frustration to God. We get mad at ourselves because we don't measure up to our own—or someone else's—ridiculously high standards, and we compound the problem by berating ourselves for feeling angry. We get mad at others for just about every reason under the sun, and yet we act as if everything is fine, the way we believe good little Christians should act.

We need to give it up, this skill we've acquired in covering up our true feelings. That doesn't mean we should lash out at the world around us, but it does mean that we should be honest with God about the causes of despair and hopelessness in our lives. If he's the cause—if you think he has reneged on one of his promises—tell him what you think. He can handle it, and once he shows you where you're wrong, as he most certainly will, you can watch your anger dissipate. The same for the other sources of rage in your life: vent your frustrations in prayer to God, and watch them evaporate before your eyes.

After you do, be prepared to add a new item to your wardrobe—a garment of praise. That's what God promises in exchange for that spirit of despair you've been wearing for far too long. Praise will never feel as good as it does when you've relieved yourself of the burden of a load of resentment God never intended you to carry in the first place.

————

Lord, I give you my tendency toward despair and depression. I know I need to express my anger instead of turning it inward, allowing it to do hidden damage in my spirit. Protect me from senselessly doing more harm than good in my misguided attempts to "behave" properly.

11

This Is the Way

Whether you turn to the right or to the left, your ears will hear a voice behind you, saying, "This is the way; walk in it."

Isaiah 30:21

FEW promises are as comforting as those that apply to the direction we seek for our lives. Others that are seemingly more dramatic come to our rescue in times of tragedy, illness, or trauma, and they provide much-needed immediate comfort. But those that assure that we are on the right track are the ones we need on a regular basis, because few concerns are as disconcerting as the nagging sensation that we have somehow missed the boat. Those promises provide ongoing comfort that we haven't missed it.

This voice assures us that God not only talks to us but also offers us a clear sense of direction. Whether we have come to a complete and puzzling stop at a crossroads or we are traveling along a road that seems to be heading in the right direction, we can count on God to let us know which way we should go.

Our responsibility—and we always have one—is to learn to recognize his voice and stay tuned in to it at all times. Listening to the wrong voice will almost certainly lead us in the wrong direction, and failing to remain alert to God's voice will cause us to miss his will completely.

But how can we know God's voice? How can we be sure his is the one speaking to us at any given moment? One way, of course, is to compare what he says to the truth of Scripture, since we know God would never lead us to do something contrary to what the Bible says. Proverbs 15:22 tells us, "Plans fail for lack of counsel, but with many advisers they succeed." In fact, scattered throughout Proverbs are verses that underscore the wisdom in seeking counsel from godly people: "The way of a fool seems right to him, but a wise man listens to advice" (12:15); "Pride only breeds quarrels, but wisdom is found in those who take advice" (13:10); "Listen to advice and accept instruction, and in the end you will be wise" (19:20); "Make plans by seeking advice" (20:18). We can also check such factors as our own motivation: Do I want to go in this direction purely for selfish reasons? Am I really hearing God, or is this merely a case of wishful thinking?

Deep down, we usually know what God is saying to us. The problem comes when we don't want to look that far, or listen that closely. We would be so much better off if we would look in our hearts first, *before* we make another mistake, *before* we have a chance to talk ourselves into going in a different direction, *before* we give other voices a chance to speak.

As you hold on to this promise, remember to do your part. Ask God to teach you to hear his voice, and then keep your ears open. You never know when he has something to tell you, such as whether the way you're going is really his will—or someone else's plan entirely.

———

Thank you, Lord, for speaking to me and leading me in the way I should go. I know that I can always trust you to steer me in the right direction. Protect me from listening to the wrong voices—or giving in to my own selfish concerns.

12

Life Everlasting

For God so loved the world that he gave his one and only Son, that whoever believes in him shall not perish but have eternal life.

John 3:16

JOHN 3:16 has to be the most quoted verse in the entire Bible. It has become so familiar that it's often easy to ignore, except at sports events when a fan behind home plate or the end zone holds up a placard bearing the ubiquitous Scripture reference.

But the promise contained in this verse is nothing to be ignored. Nor is the truth inherent in the first part of the verse—the truth that God's love is so immense, so far-reaching, so deep, that he sacrificed his one and only Son so that the rest of us could live forever in the glory of his presence. Imagine sacrificing your only child for a bunch of rebellious, ungrateful people. That kind of love is unfathomable.

As to the promise, the prospect of eternal life is equally difficult for us to comprehend. Infinity is not exactly a simple concept, especially for a people as time-bound as we are. We even speak of it in disparaging terms—"That meeting seemed to last an eternity!"—as if nothing could be more boring than an endless existence. But whatever eternity is, you can be sure that it won't be boring—not when God is in charge.

Look at the way the *Amplified Bible* treats the promise portion of John 3:16: ". . . so that whoever believes in (trusts in, clings to, relies on) him shall not perish (come to destruction, be lost) but have eternal (everlasting) life." The alternatives are clear: come to destruction or have eternal life. There's no third choice. It doesn't matter whether or not we understand eternity; we certainly understand destruction, and it's a fairly safe assumption that none of us wants to find out what that feels like.

Our inability to fully grasp—or appreciate—a specific promise in no way nullifies it. God has given us his Word, and he's sticking to it. The choice is ours: cling to Jesus Christ, rely on him, trust in him, believe in him, and spend eternity in the glorious presence of God Almighty; or deny Jesus, along with the sacrificial love of the Father, and perish, be lost, be destroyed—forever cut off from the infinite promises of God.

Let this be the one promise that you claim above all others. Think of it as priority one; your ability to access and claim all the other promises in the Bible hinges on this one verse of Scripture.

———

Lord, don't ever let this verse become so familiar to me that I lose its precious meaning along with its precious promise. Thank you for your offer of eternal life, and thank you for making the supreme sacrifice on my behalf: giving up the life of your Son so that I may live throughout eternity with you.

13

Fearless Fighter

For God did not give us a spirit of timidity, but a spirit of power, of love and of self-discipline.

2 Timothy 1:7

By all indications, Timothy was in a tough spot. Paul's son in the faith, who had labored with the apostle for more than fifteen years, was facing the biggest challenge of his young life: Timothy was about to inherit Paul's mantle of leadership among the far-flung congregations of the early church. Timothy no doubt had his share of concerns about this new direction his life was taking. Would the churches recognize his authority? Was he equal to the task of carrying on Paul's work? And how would he manage without his mentor?

Paul seems to have had his own concerns about Timothy's current spiritual condition. Scattered throughout this letter are words of both admonition and encouragement. Among the strongest is the reminder expressed as a promise in verse 7. You can be assured, Paul wrote, that if you are experiencing fear, the accompanying spirit of timidity—or cowardice—is not from God. Instead, what God gives is a spirit of power, love, and self-discipline. That last word can also be translated into such terms as *calmness, self-control,* and *a sound mind*—hardly the qualities of a fearful person. In the same spirit, Paul later encouraged Timothy to conduct himself as a soldier of Christ.

Paul's words must have had their intended effect, because Timothy went on to serve the church well in Paul's place. It was more than mere words, of course, that made the difference; it was the power in the promise behind the words. Few things in the world can dramatically change a shy person into a fearless fighter, but we have several millennia of evidence that the Spirit of God is a master at making such transformations.

What God did for Timothy—and a group of frightened disciples who hunkered down after the Crucifixion and came out fighting after the Resurrection—he will do for you. Your fears, whether real or imagined, are real to you, and you need to understand that there's no way those emotions have invaded your life courtesy of your loving heavenly Father. He offers the antidote to fear: the Holy Spirit of God, who transforms your timidity into courage.

As you read your Bible, pay special attention to those instances in which confidence replaced panic and changed lives. The same power that God made available to his people in biblical times is available to you today—you have only to ask for it.

———

Lord, I know that my fears are not from you. I give you my fears in exchange for the spirit of power, love, and self-discipline that you have promised in your Word. Thank you for transforming my cowardice into courage.

14

Unmerited Favor

But to each one of us grace has been given as Christ apportioned it.

Ephesians 4:7

I F we could reduce the gospel of Jesus Christ to a single word, that word would be *grace*. Often defined as "God's unmerited favor," grace represents the gift of salvation that God freely gives to humankind—sinful, ungrateful, unworthy humankind. And despite our very human tendency to think that everything in the world revolves around us, the grace of God happens to be one thing that we in no way influence. We can't earn it, we don't deserve it, and yet he gives it to us.

Meanwhile, the world keeps telling us, usually through television commercials hawking something we have to pay for, what we *do* deserve: an extended vacation on some remote island paradise, a luxury car that costs more than our first house, a shiny and healthy head of hair without a single gray strand to be found. Most of all, of course, we deserve a break today.

What we actually deserve is what everyone throughout history has earned—absolutely nothing, unless you want to get into issues such as condemnation, judgment, hellfire, and the like. The truth is, in the overall scheme of redemption, humankind has done zero to merit the kindness of God. We've rejected him, snubbed our noses at him, turned our backs on him—except when we need something, that is—and generally treated him as a doddering old servant. We haven't exactly been stellar examples of kindness requited.

But God keeps at it, continuing to offer his free gift of grace to the very people who do him wrong. He extends his grace not only through the forgiveness of sins but also through the acts of justification—treating individuals as if they had never sinned—and reconciliation—closing the gap that sin has created between God and individuals. If grace seems to be too good to be true, well, in any realm besides the kingdom of God, it certainly is.

While there's nothing you can do to earn God's grace, there are plenty of ways in which you can respond to his gift appropriately, such as accepting it gratefully, showing your gratitude through your obedience, maintaining fellowship with God, and serving him and other people with a sacrificial joy. Is all that necessary? No. Is there anything you can do to receive a greater measure of grace? No. Grace is a gift with no strings attached. And you don't even have to pay for it—unlike that expensive vacation, that luxury car, that new-and-improved hair color, that trip to McDonald's. Grace is on the house—God's house.

———

Thank you, Lord, for not giving me what I deserve. It does seem too good to be true, but by faith I believe that you have made this offer to me, and I gratefully accept your free gift of grace.

15

My Father's House

In my Father's house are many rooms; if it were not so, I would have told you. I am going there to prepare a place for you. And if I go and prepare a place for you, I will come back and take you to be with me that you also may be where I am.

John 14:2–3

Aₛₖ any ten people what they think heaven is like, and I guarantee you will get ten completely different answers. Some people imagine heaven to be much the way movies depict it: kind of dreamy, ethereal, misty, and white—always white. Other people carry with them into adulthood a very childlike image of heaven, a place where winged angelic beings sit on puffy clouds and play harps throughout eternity. Others—and these would be the people who figure they have no hope of ending up there—see heaven as a place where there's no fun, no friends, no partying, just a great big eternal yawn. And then there are those people who have at least a passing familiarity with the Bible, and they know that heaven will be a place of glory, an eternity spent in the presence of God.

And still, no two answers will be identical.

There are good reasons for that, mainly that no one knows what heaven is *really* like until he or she arrives there, and then it's a bit too late to write a book describing its many wonders. The Bible offers clues, and plenty of scholars have devoted good portions of their lives in trying to unravel the mystery that heaven is, but few agree about it.

Heaven, it seems, is one more truth we have to accept on faith. But what a truth it is! If nothing else, we know that heaven is the dimension in which God "dwells," even though he is omnipresent, or present everywhere. Psalm 139:7–10 expresses his omnipresence in this way: "Where can I go from your Spirit? Where can I flee from your presence? If I go up to the heavens, you are there; if I make my bed in the depths, you are there. If I rise on the wings of the dawn, if I settle on the far side of the sea, even there your hand will guide me, your right hand will hold me fast."

We also know that it is a place of perfection and incomparable beauty. In Revelation 21, the Bible describes the new heaven, the place where the righteous will dwell, as a city that shines with God's glory much like a crystal jewel. "It had a great, high wall with twelve gates, and with twelve angels at the gates," wrote the Apostle John in verse 12. "The wall was made of jasper, and the city of pure gold, as pure as glass . . . The twelve gates were twelve pearls, each gate made of a single pearl. The street of the city was of pure gold, like transparent glass" (verses 18, 21). It's a place of freedom, peace, security, and everlasting joy. But we can probably best describe heaven by listing what will *not* be present there, such as sorrow, pain, darkness, sin, depression, despair, hatred, shame, and a host of other negatives.

Right now, as the verse in John 14:3 promises, Jesus is in heaven, in his Father's house, preparing a place especially for you. For *you.* It's a bit much to take in, to be sure, but it's right there in Scripture.

What's more, he promises to come back to take you there so you can be with him forever. And that, after all, is what heaven is all about.

————

Lord, I cannot begin to imagine all that you have prepared for us in heaven. All I know is that it's going to be glorious, because we will be forever in the presence of your glory. Keep me grounded on earth but looking forward to the hope of heaven.

16

"I Have Called You Friends"

I no longer call you servants, because a servant does not know his master's business. Instead, I have called you friends, for everything that I learned from my Father I have made known to you.

John 15:15

If you have, or ever have had, a true friend, you know what a treasure such a person can be. Just think of all he or she has meant to your life: a true friend stands by your side through the bad times as well as the good, forgives you when you say or do hurtful things, shares both material possessions and spiritual wisdom with you, and keeps you from doing some really stupid things. A true friend loves you no matter what.

It may be difficult to comprehend, but Jesus Christ has called you his friend. By sharing the spiritual truth that once only God knew, Jesus has brought you into the inner circle. That act alone is proof positive that you are more than a servant—and you aren't even required to understand all that he has revealed to you. No one can, and no one does.

But because you have believed the essence of what was revealed to you, that Jesus is the Messiah, the Son of God, you now have the kind of relationship with the Lord that Abraham had with God. Abraham, whom James 2:23 called "God's friend," enjoyed an unusual level of access to God the Father; likewise, you have a similar degree of access to him. As Jesus' friend, you enjoy privileges beyond compare, and intimacy with God is just one of them.

Maybe you are at a place in your life when friends have become hard to find. Perhaps someone has betrayed you, or you left all your friends behind when you moved to a new area, or a close friend has passed away. And maybe the thought of having a friend that you can't even see doesn't exactly cut it with you right now. You feel as if you need a flesh-and-blood friend, someone who can give you a hug when you need it most.

If you let him, Jesus can become to you all that a true companion could possibly be—and far more. Turn to Jesus and begin to see him as the Friend he already is: someone who has already laid down his life for you, has promised never to leave or abandon you, and, in fact, has promised to come back and take you home to live with him forever. This is beginning to sound like the kind of friend you could probably use right now—and always. Because you will never find a truer friend than Jesus.

————

Lord, I thank you for bringing me into your circle of friends. When I begin to feel sorry for myself, thinking that my companions have abandoned me, remind me that you are the truest friend I will ever have.

17

Overtaken by Blessing

If you fully obey the LORD your God and carefully follow all his commands I give you today, the LORD your God will set you high above all the nations on earth. All these blessings will come upon you and accompany you if you obey the LORD your God.

Deuteronomy 28:1–2

L IKE many promises in the Bible, this is one God made to a specific group of people at a specific time. In this case, the promise applied to the personal relationship between God and Israel; God promised that if the Israelites chose to be in the right relationship with him, then blessings would accompany them—or *overtake* them, as some Bible versions translate the thought. If the Israelites refused to enter into the covenant relationship God offered, they could expect curses.

In this passage, Moses clearly laid out the blessings God promised: prominence over every other nation, respect among the nations, victory over Israel's enemies, commercial and financial prosperity, fruitfulness, abundance—even weather favorable to an agrarian society ("rain on your land in season," v. 12). The Israelites would be known as the people of God—both a witness to God's goodness and a testimony to the awesome power behind their nation.

What did God require from Israel? Simple obedience—not as a means of "earning" God's blessings but as an indication of their genuine faith in and faithfulness to him.

So how does this promise apply to you? First, it applies with regard to your standing as a child of God in the coming kingdom, the one Jesus Christ established after his ascension (Eph. 1:20–23). Israel's special status as a chosen nation, as well as the religious observances and rituals God mandated, served as a prophetic example of the kingdom that Jesus would introduce. The blessings promised to Israel, though, are but a mere shadow of those to come; they will no doubt overtake you, if not overwhelm you.

The second way this promise applies to you is with regard to the blessings you can expect to enjoy now, as an obedient, faithful member of the family of God here on Earth. That's because the principle that undergirds the promise in Deuteronomy 28 applies on a personal level as well: show your faith in God through your obedience, and you can expect God's blessings to come upon and accompany you.

A multitude of Bible verses that relate to blessings such as prosperity, abundance, and victory serve to confirm the personal nature of the promises. Verses relating to material and spiritual prosperity are scattered throughout the Bible. "'I know the plans I have for you,'" declares the LORD, "'plans to prosper you and not to harm you, plans to give you hope and a future'" (Jer. 29:11); the wisdom books in particular offer numerous references to prosperity (see Job 22:21, 42:10; Ps. 1:3, 128:2; and Prov. 3:2, 8:18, 11:25, 13:21, 16:20, 19:8, 21:21, 28:13, 28:25). The blessings of abundance cover such things as food (Ps. 36:8, Ps. 132:15, Prov. 12:11, Job 36:31); clothing (Isa. 23:18); peace and security (Jer. 33:6,9); God's goodness (Ps. 145:7); grace (Rom. 5:17, 1 Tim. 1:14); and general prosperity (Deut. 28:11, Josh. 17:14; Ps. 65:11; Jer. 31:14; and Matt. 13:12). And as for victory, 1 Corinthians 15:57 assures us that "He gives us the victory through our Lord Jesus Christ." It's the Lord who always gives us the victory, no matter what our earthly weapons are (see Ps. 138:35, 44:3–7, 108:13 and Prov. 2:7, 21:31).

God did not restrict his promises to the future; you can access them today as you walk in obedience to his Word.

———

Lord, I want to know what it means to be overtaken by your promises. Grant me the grace to remain obedient and faithful to you, never wavering in my faith in what you have promised.

18

Watch Him Flee

Submit yourselves, then, to God. Resist the devil, and he will flee from you.

James 4:7

THERE you are, face-to-face with the unseen enemy, the big one, the devil himself. Like a twenty-first-century Bruce Lee—or Buffy, the TV vampire slayer—you kick, punch, slam, and make all sorts of impressive moves. Your every shot lands right where you aimed it. You're so effective, so successful, that Satan cowers and slinks off to find some lesser mortal to pick on.

Hold it. Check out what James 4:7 says again. It says nothing about dealing a hammer blow to the enemy or engaging in one-on-one combat with the devil. What it promises is that the devil will flee—run away, retreat, skedaddle, make a break for it—and all you have to do is resist him. But why does he flee? Are you all that frightening? Does Satan, not to mention his many minions, tremble at the very sight of you? Not quite. It's the presence of our always victorious Lord that causes him to fear for his life, such as it is.

Look at the rest of the verse. The promise takes effect when we have completely submitted ourselves to God. Without God, we are puny weaklings. We can rant and rave at the enemy until we're ready to collapse, but he'll just stand his ground, mocking, jeering, and making a demonic nuisance of himself.

Resistance implies a force pushing against something. When that force is Satan, and that something is you, you can be sure he'll be pushing hard. How will you handle that? Will you recall the promise of God?

Remember: you don't have to fight back. God has become your shield and rampart (Ps. 91:4), an impenetrable wall that does not give way no matter how much force comes against it. Think Fort Knox, only stronger, much, much stronger. Add an invisible barrier of supernatural magnetic energy, a fail-safe repellent that sends invading marauders in the opposite direction, and you have the perfect formula for resistance.

When you genuinely submit to God, you relinquish to him all control over your life. You say to the Father, as Jesus did, "Yet not as I will, but as you will" (Matt. 26:39). In doing that, you give God permission to fight your battles for you. In fact, the word translated as "submit" in the original Greek implies being under the command and authority of a military leader. When you do this, you step aside and allow God, your Commander in Chief, to stand between you and your enemy, whether that enemy be Satan or a flesh-and-blood person. You can be assured that his invisible shield will offer all the resistance you will ever need.

———

Lord, even though I can't see it, I trust that your shield of protection stands between me and the forces of darkness that would love to bring me down. Help me to resist Satan when he comes to harass me. I humbly submit my will to yours.

19

A Good Measure

Give, and it will be given to you. A good measure, pressed down, shaken together and running over, will be poured into your lap. For with the measure you use, it will be measured to you.

Luke 6:38

FOR modern-day people unfamiliar with the ways in which first-century merchants conducted business, the meaning of this verse—especially the second sentence—may be a bit obscure. "Give, and it will be given to you" we understand just fine, but the rest, well, we sort of skim over that part. But to Jesus' contemporaries, the illustration was a vivid one.

Grain merchants at the time were expected to err on the side of the customer; to make sure they did not shortchange anyone, they would fill their customers' baskets until the grain began to overflow. Devout Jewish merchants in particular adhered to this practice. As in any society, though, some had figured out ways to cheat their customers. And then there were the rare gems, those merchants who were so generous that they would press the grain down into the baskets and still fill them to overflowing. *Their* customers walked away particularly happy.

The meaning was clear to those in Jesus' audience: if you give to others with letter-of-the-law honesty, that's what you can expect in return. But if you give with a heart that overflows with generosity, you can expect an equally abundant return. Woe to those, of course, whose dealings are tainted with dishonesty and stinginess; their return will be skimpy indeed.

Even the image of the overflow being "poured into your lap" is one that would have resonated with everyone within hearing distance of Jesus' words. To those people, "lap" referred to one of two things: a long, tunic-type robe worn over their regular garments to carry the overflow of grain, or a large, pocketlike fold of cloth in which people carried their valuables and other personal possessions. Instead of merely catching the overflow from the basket, Jesus said, the overflow would be "poured" into that piece of cloth—hardly the image of a smattering of grains falling out of the basket.

Jesus, of course, was not merely directing his comments to merchants. He wanted, and wants, his followers to be generous with others to the point of blessing them beyond their needs. Your generosity will not go unnoticed; the Lord is well aware of every overflowing "grain"—time, money, effort, material goods—that you give away. God promises you *will* get your reward—and from that, you can continue to give to overflowing. Try as you might, you can't outgive God. But trying to can be a whole lot of fun.

————

Lord, let me never be stingy or dishonest in my giving to you and to others. Create in me a heart that overflows with generosity, one that wants to bless others by sharing the abundance that you have given to me. And if that same measure is given to me, I will have only you to thank.

20

Mountain-Moving Faith

Then the disciples came to Jesus in private and asked, "Why couldn't we drive [the demon] out?"

He replied, "Because you have so little faith. I tell you the truth, if you have faith as small as a mustard seed, you can say to this mountain, 'Move from here to there' and it will move. Nothing will be impossible for you."

Matthew 17:19–20

Has anyone ever challenged you about the truth expressed in this verse? You make an innocent remark about the kind of faith it takes to move a mountain, and some wise guy comes along with a dare: "Oh, yeah? You think faith can move mountains? Well, then, go right ahead—make Everest move. Just an inch. I'm waiting!"

Explaining figurative speech can become so tiresome, can't it? First the mustard seed, then the mountain—it makes you wonder how Jesus put up with the literalists of his day. You question whether some of the people who claimed to have found his parables so puzzling weren't just being stubborn.

Jesus, of course, was making a statement about the disciples' lack of faith and all that they could accomplish if they would just learn to exercise even a small measure of it. Apparently, in John 17 the disciples were trying their hands at exorcism, and in their own strength at that. So this poor guy, the father of the demon-possessed child, had to muster up his own faith once again and beg Jesus to do what his disciples could not. You can almost see Jesus throwing his arms up in frustration. He rebuked the demon, forced it to leave, and healed the child.

When Jesus was on Earth, he made it clear that his power came from God the Father. And he made it clear that the same power he had was available to his followers. He did not do anything for that child that the disciples themselves could not have done—if they'd had only the tiniest amount of genuine faith.

We are in the same position as the disciples. Power is ours for the asking. But we negate the promise expressed in this portion of Scripture in any number of ways. We ask for things that are clearly outside God's will for us ("Make my wife leave me so I can marry someone else!"). We place our faith in our *faith* rather than in our *God*. We treat God as if he is a genie in a bottle who must grant us our three wishes.

Go to God with your mustard-seed faith. Place it before him and ask him to accomplish both great and small things that will bring honor and glory to his name. Make that mountain-moving promise real in your life by simply believing that God will do what he has said he will do.

———

Lord, I confess that sometimes I place my faith in everything but you. And sometimes I ask for the wrong things, in the wrong way. Teach me to exercise my mustard-seed faith in a way that is pleasing to you—and a way that will make those mountains move after all.

21

Do What?

But you will receive power when the Holy Spirit comes on you; and you will be my witnesses in Jerusalem, and in all Judea and Samaria, and to the ends of the earth.

Acts 1:8

You've got to hand it to the disciples. They were nothing if not a resilient lot. They watched as their Lord, their Messiah, suffered an agonizing death on a criminal's cross, and they figured they were next. So they basically headed for the hills until three days later, when Jesus rose from the grave and started making personal appearances to his followers. They barely got used to having him back when he started talking about leaving again.

So what did he choose as his final words to these already bewildered folks? The words recorded in Acts 1:8, promising them that they would proclaim the good news of salvation to the ends of the earth. Granted, there was that part about the power of the Holy Spirit coming on them, but they weren't in any condition to try to figure out what that was all about. And then, just like that, Jesus was gone again, taken up into the clouds and carried away out of their sight.

Whew! Imagine what a whirlwind the disciples must have felt they were living in! And then they were supposed to tell others what they had witnessed over the previous three years? Some of them had to be thinking, *Uh, I don't think so.*

That kind of thinking is not limited to the disciples who knew Jesus personally. Down through the centuries, many believers have thought the same thing—sometimes due to the threat of unspeakable forms of persecution and even death; at other times because of the fear of rejection; and at still other times because of their natural shyness. In any event, it's never easy to speak up when you know you're likely to be put down.

But unlike the disciples on the day of Jesus' Ascension, those who have lived since then know what eventually happened. The Holy Spirit came and brought the promise of empowerment, including the courage to witness.

Do you believe you can receive the power of the Holy Spirit? Then you can access the confidence to share the good news of salvation with others. Does that mean you'll end up on a street corner, handing out tracts and wearing a sandwich board that reads "Repent!"? No—unless you feel an incredibly strong call to do that. All God asks you to do is to be yourself and rely on the promised Holy Spirit to show you how and when to share your faith with others. His power is fine-tuned and highly sensitive. He will guide you in the witnessing way that best suits you.

———

Lord, I do want to be able to witness with greater boldness. Teach me to rely on the Holy Spirit's power, and release me from the fear that the Spirit will require me to evangelize in a way that I find uncomfortable.

22

Godly Character

But the fruit of the Spirit is love, joy, peace, patience, kindness, good-ness, faithfulness, gentleness and self-control. Against such things there is no law.

Galatians 5:22–23

CONTRARY to what some of us seem to think, this list of the fruit of the Spirit is not a type of spiritual scorecard. Too many of us use it in that way, judging ourselves on our daily behavior: *Well, you did okay today on the love and joy, but wow! You have got to do some-thing about patience and self-control!* Even worse, some believers act as if God is the one keeping score, tallying up our grades in preparation for that one big final exam: "Right now you have a C in faith-fulness. If you expect to spend eternity with me, you'll have to work extra hard to pull that grade up to at least a B!"

Seems foolish, doesn't it? But many of us make the mistake of treating these nine qualities as if they're categories we need to work on. We should know better, especially once we realize that Paul in-tentionally used the singular word "fruit" instead of the plural *fruits*.

He was trying to get us to see that these qualities work together as a cohesive unit.

Taken together, the characteristics he listed define life in the Spirit. These qualities require no law to govern or produce them, because they flow from the Spirit of God and represent the freedom found in the Christian life—not the bondage found in the Law. They stand in complete contrast to the list of the works of the flesh found in the previous verses (Gal. 5:19–21).

The key to acquiring and possessing these characteristics appears in verse 16: "So I say, live by the Spirit, and you will not gratify the desires of sinful nature." This involves habitually submitting to the control of the Holy Spirit; it's a way of living, not a one-time decision. As you yield to the Holy Spirit, he produces fruit in your life: a godly, self-sacrificial love; a lasting joy that does not depend on circumstances; a deep, abiding peace that we cannot understand; an uncommon patience with God, with others, and with ourselves; a compassionate and tender kindness; a spiritual and moral goodness; an unwavering faithfulness; a humble and submissive gentleness; and an unusual measure of self-control.

It's time to stop keeping score and start living in the Spirit. Grades don't count when it comes to the fruit of the Spirit; all that counts is your willingness to submit to the Spirit's control and allow him to produce his qualities in your life. On your own, you'll never produce a crop as sweet and lasting and abundant as the harvest he has the power to produce.

———

Lord, I want these qualities in my life. Teach me how to live by the Spirit, so my character may reflect the fruit of the Spirit.

23

Loving the Unlovable

No one has ever seen God; but if we love one another, God lives in us and his love is made complete in us.

1 John 4:12

THE Bible speaks often of brotherly love—or whatever phrase is in current use in this day of gender-neutral terms. What the term refers to is the love of one Christian for another that makes us valid witnesses to the love of Christ. But sometimes it's just plain hard to love others in the family of God. Some of our brothers and sisters can be downright annoying, infuriating, exasperating—not at all like us, of course.

To deny that loving others is possible, though, is to deny the truth of Scripture, because love for our fellow believers is a theme that is repeated throughout the New Testament. It's a truth that we often have to accept by faith alone, especially when we come up against someone who in our estimation is decidedly unlovable.

Look at it this way: God, who is the very embodiment of love, created us in his image; we therefore have the capacity not only to love but also to love everyone, as God does. God came to Earth in a man named Jesus, manifesting his love in human form. Those of us who have received God into our lives have the Spirit dwelling within us, and since God is love . . . well, you get the picture. God's love is "made complete" in us as we demonstrate our love for one another.

This is a powerful promise. Because no one has seen God at any time, love makes us the embodiment of who he is. For many people, the only evidence of the love of God may be us—the way we treat others, the kindness, compassion, tolerance, and patience we exhibit toward others. That's a daunting thought, but God assures us through John's Epistle that this is the way it is.

Think about that the next time Sister Doris grates on your nerves or Brother Don pushes your buttons. God has promised not only that you can care for those people but also that his character will be apparent through the love you demonstrate for all the Dorises and Dons in your life. Learning to love the seemingly unlovable is a small price to pay in exchange for such a payoff, the tangible evidence of God's love in the world.

———

Lord, you know how hard it is for me to love certain people—or even to act as if I do. I ask you to give me your love, the only true love anyway, for those people, so that I might play my small part in showing the world that you are alive and well on planet Earth.

24

Total Renovation

Therefore, if anyone is in Christ, he is a new creation; the old has gone, the new has come!

2 Corinthians 5:17

Do you get the feeling that Paul was just a bit excited when he wrote this? And why shouldn't he have been? His new life in Christ came upon him so dramatically that anything less than wholehearted enthusiasm would have seemed ungrateful. The old in his life—his persecution of the new sect of Christ-followers—was gone; the new—a total embrace and recognition of Christ as the long-awaited Messiah—had come! He probably wanted to shout it from the housetops, and possibly did.

Hold it, you say, if you have more than a passing knowledge of the life of Paul. *Isn't this the same guy who got into a tiff with one of his fellow workers (Acts 15:39) and who sometimes came across as, well, arrogant? And you say he was a new creation?*

Yes. He was. And so are all of us who are "in Christ"—born anew into the family of God. Becoming a new creation does not mean that we become perfect. We are still human beings, with all the potential for sinful actions and attitudes that being human involves. What has become new is our perspective, our way of looking, thinking, acting, and being.

In theological terms, this promise of new life is called the doctrine of regeneration. The power of the Holy Spirit gives new life to the believer at the moment the person first responds to God's offer of salvation. This new, divine life is what makes possible the believer's increasing conformity to the image of Christ, as the person shelves his former belief system, values, lifestyle, and plans in favor of a revised, godly perspective on life.

To be in Christ means to share his nature. Your motivations, behavior, attitudes, thought life—in fact, the very heartbeat of your life—increasingly become more like his. God instantaneously imparted your new life in Christ to you, but your adjustment to this new pattern of living occurs throughout your lifetime. So if you're not exactly feeling like a new creation, take heart: the fact is that you can experience the reality of that promise a little more each day, as you allow yourself to become more and more conformed to the image of Christ. The old truly has gone, more than you may realize. And the new truly has come, probably *much* more than you realize.

———

Lord, thank you for making me a new creation, whether I feel like one today or not. Continue to replace the remnants of my old way of life with the reality of the new way of life that you have promised to me; change my heart and mind to conform to the image of Jesus Christ.

25

Enjoying God

Delight yourself in the LORD
and he will give you the desires of your heart.

Psalm 37:4

W HAT are the true desires of your heart? Not the material things you may want, that superficial layer of wishful thinking that tends to obscure your genuine desires. That layer represents things you believe are attainable and therefore safe to think about. Sweep it away, and you unearth those things you truly desire, the ones that are too painful to think about because you still see them as unattainable. These may include loving and being loved; having a faithful, intimate friend; being free from worry and despair; finding out what it would be like not to feel lonely all the time.

Those are the true desires of your heart, aren't they? The rest of it, the things that make for safe conversation, is just a smoke screen designed to keep the hurt from showing. That smoke screen also prevents you from exposing those desires to God, the only one who can make them a reality in your life. It's time to lift the screen and ask God to search your heart for even more desires, the ones that dwell so deep inside of you that you've obscured them from your own view.

Pay close attention now, because this is where most of us get it wrong. This promise, the promise that God will grant you the desires of your heart, does come with a condition. The condition appears in the first word of this verse: "delight." Did you get that? The word is not obey, worship, serve, praise, genuflect, prostrate yourself on a cold, hard floor in humble submission to the Almighty after fasting for three weeks and sleeping on a bed of nails. Sure, all those things are well and good—most of them, at least—but this promise encourages us to do something significantly different, and that's *delight* ourselves in the Lord.

Enjoying God—taking pleasure in him, in being with him, in basking in the glow of his glorious presence. How many of us do that on anything resembling a regular basis? Well, how many of us have received the desires of our hearts? After all, there *is* a correlation between the condition and the fulfillment of the promise.

Does that mean that God is stubbornly holding out on us, refusing to give us the desires of our heart until we get our act together and enjoy him? It would be difficult to delight ourselves in him if that were the case. No, what this verse implies is that our enjoyment of God becomes the very embodiment of the desires of our heart. When we do one, we already have the other.

––––––––

Lord, show me how you want me to delight in you. Give me the grace to simply be *in your presence, not performing any religious duties, not doing what I think I should* do, *just enjoying the pleasure of your company.*

26

Sounds in the Night

So do not fear, for I am with you;
do not be dismayed, for I am your God.
I will strengthen you and help you;
I will uphold you with my righteous right hand.

Isaiah 41:10

IN *Reflections for Ragamuffins,* author and Episcopal priest Brennan Manning wrote of a certain method Native Americans once used in training boys to become fearless men. As soon as a boy turned thirteen, he was taken to the middle of a forest. The denser the woods and the vegetation, the better. And if this happened on a moonless or cloud-covered night, even better yet. The boy's tribe did not expect him to find his way out; all he had to do was remain there, alone, all night long, listening to every big and little sound the woods would make.[1]

If you've ever done much off-trail camping, you know how noisy the woods can get at night. Leaves rustle, branches snap, owls hoot, and you've got to wonder what crickets do all day, because they sure make a racket all night. But worst of all are the unidentifiable sounds, the ones that you just know are attached to mountain lions, grizzly bears, rattlesnakes, and all kinds of creatures from the black lagoon.

Sure, these young boys had to put up a brave front, but fears tend to surface when you're alone, no matter who you are. Imagine the boy's relief when dawn finally broke! And that's when he realized he had no need to fear, because there was his father, armed with bow and arrow, right where he had been all night: hidden from view but protecting his son.

The lesson for us is obvious. Even in the midst of our deepest fears, our darkest nights, our densest worries, there is God, right where he's been all along. "I am with you," he says, and we fail to remember that when we most need to. "I am your God," he adds, and we think, *Yes, of course,* and go right on acting as if he isn't. "I will strengthen you and help you," he continues, and we want details on how he plans to do that. "I will uphold you with my righteous right hand," he concludes, and we want to inspect that hand to make sure it's strong enough.

God is clear on his resolve to protect us from internal fears and external dangers, even if we are not. We really should take him at his word, especially when it's dark and scary and we feel as if we are all alone. Yes, we'll see him when the light breaks through, but we'd be much better off if we trusted in his promise and presence throughout those long nights.

———

Lord, thank you for always being with me and always being my God. I believe that you will strengthen me and help me and uphold me whenever I am afraid and in danger.

27

Case Dismissed

Let the wicked forsake his way and the evil man his thoughts. Let him turn to the LORD, and he will have mercy on him, and to our God, for he will freely pardon.

Isaiah 55:7

If you've ever been on the receiving end of God's mercy and compassion—and you have, whether you realize it or not—you know what an awesome gift that can be. We most keenly experience these qualities when we deserve them the least, when we've committed some egregious sin that we know warrants severe punishment. God realizes that we've done such a fine job of punishing ourselves that he says, "Enough. No more punishment. Not from me—and not from yourself. It's over."

We often see human examples of this in the courtroom, of all places. A judge presiding over the case of a child killed in a car accident refuses to continue with the prosecution of the parents. She's within her legal rights to pursue the charges, because the parents failed to secure the child properly in her car seat. But they're good parents; they thought the strap was fastened; they had no history of neglect; they are clearly distraught. She announces her ruling: "The parents have suffered enough. All charges are dropped. Case dismissed."

That's where the similarity between human and divine mercy ends, though. The judge goes on to the next case. God, however, stays with the parents, comforting them, consoling them—and eventually, over time, turning their mourning into joy.

The Bible has much to say about God's mercy. It never fails; it is "from everlasting to everlasting" (Ps. 103:17, NKJV). What's more, God is "rich in mercy" (Eph. 2:4), and that means he has plenty to give away. And because it is an aspect of his love, he *wants* to extend it to us. He decides "on whom [he] will have mercy . . . and compassion" (Ex. 33:19), but because these attributes flow from his goodness and love, we have the confidence that he will offer them to those who turn their hearts toward him.

Look at some biblical examples of God's mercy. Back when he was known as Saul, the Apostle Paul certainly deserved God's wrath. He thought he was doing the right thing by persecuting the Jewish followers of Christ, but God set him straight. It was Jesus—God himself—whom Paul was persecuting (Acts 9:4–5). Yet God had mercy on him and eventually transformed him into a powerful leader in the early church.

And long before Paul, King David got himself into such a royal mess that God sent a prophet to set him straight (see 2 Samuel 11–12). Nathan made it clear that by committing adultery with Bathsheba, impregnating her, and sending her husband to his death, David had displeased God, to put it mildly. David suffered the consequences—his first child by Bathsheba died—but God soon after blessed them with another child and continued to bless David throughout his reign.

Even if we had no other reason to fall on our knees in gratitude before the Most High God, the promise of his mercy and compassion alone would be enough. When we stop and think of all the times he probably should have locked us away, covered us with boils, or otherwise struck us down because of our sin and rebellion, we have to marvel at the utter kindness of God. We deserve so much worse than we ever get. We are a fortunate people indeed.

––––––––

Lord, I am so grateful to you for the many times you have dealt with me in a merciful way. I know I have deserved your divine retribution and wrath, and yet you have shown me your love and kindness and goodness instead. Thank you for never giving me what I deserve.

28

No Expiration Date

The grass withers and the flowers fall,
but the word of our God stands forever.

Isaiah 40:8

In the verses preceding this one, the prophet Isaiah compared people to grass: Just like vegetation, people are destined to wither and
die. People are transitory; generations come, generations go; an individual may be here today and gone tomorrow. But the Word of
God, he says, will stand forever. Its permanence is guaranteed; its
promises are secure; it will endure long after everything else fades
into insignificance.

That guarantee, that promise wouldn't mean anything if we did
not believe what the Word of God says. Think about that for a while.
Would it make any difference to you if, say, the writings of some cult
leader suddenly disappeared? Of course not. You never believed
what he wrote anyway, so you don't care if his writings survive the
year, let alone eternity. In fact, you'd probably mutter a "good rid-
dance" to celebrate.

God's Word has lasting value whether you believe its contents or not, of course. But it has value *to you* only when you wholeheartedly embrace the precious truths it contains. Knowing it will "stand forever" then becomes far more than just a nice promise. The endurance of the Word of God means that he will not suddenly change the program on you. You'll never hear him say, "Oops! You know that whole plan of redemption? You can forget that now. I've decided that we'll just hold a lottery to determine who gets to spend eternity with me."

The permanence of God's Word also means that every single promise in the Bible will endure. Not one carries an expiration date this side of eternity; there's no chance that you'll ever claim a promise that's no longer valid. You don't have to worry that one day, when you finally begin to believe God's promise of an abundant life, he'll pull a fast one on you and rescind it: "John 10:10? No, no, child; that was good only through the turn of the last millennium. Sorry!"

There aren't many things in our lives that we can consider permanent. Jobs, friends, our favorite brand of toothpaste, even churches come and go. And the wisdom of the world, well, that seems to change on a daily basis; what was politically correct today may not be tomorrow, depending on which way the wind blows.

But when it comes to God—to his promises, his character, his Word, his existence, his nature—we have the assurance of knowing that none of that will ever alter or disappear. In an uncertain world, that can make all the difference in the way we live our lives.

———

Lord, I believe that every promise you made and every word you spoke in Scripture will stand forever. Thank you for providing us with something of permanence in the midst of the uncertain world in which we live.

29

Repairing a Broken Heart

The LORD is close to the brokenhearted
and saves those who are crushed in spirit.

Psalm 34:18

THIS is another two-pronged promise verse, with the second part seemingly referring to the salvation of those who have hit rock bottom, people who are so crushed in spirit that they finally get to the point of calling on the Lord. The first part, though, is for those of us who have experienced the indescribable pain of a broken heart. If you are among that group, you know full well how agonizing that pain can be.

Well-meaning friends try all kinds of things to snap you out of it and cheer you up. "She was no good for you," they say, trying to make you believe that there's someone out there who *is*. "You're better off without him!" they say, trying to make you believe that being alone is really better than being with the one you still love. Even if you agree with what those friends say, that does not reduce the pain one bit. Their words only add to your despair.

If you're truly blessed, you may have a friend who understands that no words can change the way you feel. That kind of friend is simply there for you—in your physical presence when needed, in spirit at all other times. That kind of friend knows that your suffering needs to run its course.

God is like that friend. He stays close to you, whether you sense his presence or not. He may not even try to speak to you, knowing that you may not be capable of hearing his voice just then. But he is there and always will be, regardless of the circumstances.

Maybe the relationship *was* all wrong. Maybe she *was* no good for you. Maybe you *are* better off without him. Maybe it was even a sinful situation. You know what? That doesn't matter when it comes to the pain you're in. As pleased as God is that your life may now be set back on the right course, he is still well aware of your broken heart. Unlike those insensitive souls who seem to show up at just the wrong time in our lives, God doesn't pull an "I told you so" on you.

The Lord will never turn his back on you. He will always remain close, waiting for that moment when you are finally ready to turn to him to give you the comfort you so desperately need—and to repair your broken heart. He promised.

————

Lord, I want to believe that you are close to me when I'm in deep emotional pain. I want to believe that you still care, even when my own bad choices are the cause of my anguish. Help me to believe that you will be there with me, no matter how badly I've messed things up.

30

A Wholehearted Pursuit

You will seek me and find me when you seek me with all your heart.

Jeremiah 29:13

FOR years, the prophet Jeremiah had been warning the Israelites to get their act together. After enemies had taken most into captivity in Babylon, Jeremiah continued to relate the word of the Lord to them. Jeremiah 29 records the contents of a letter he sent to the exiles, basically telling them to chill and settle down in Babylon, because they were going to be there for a while. His advice ran counter to that of the false prophets, who had predicted a quick end to the captivity. Jeremiah, of course, was eventually proven to be right. Meanwhile, in this letter he had a few things to tell the captives.

Included in his message was the assurance that they would return to Jerusalem, just not right away. And even then, their God would require their repentance. Through Jeremiah, God promised that the Israelites' rebellion and obstinacy would not separate them from him forever. But they would find him only when they sought him with their whole hearts.

Part of the message for us, of course, is that if we are in rebellion against God, we can trust that we will be able to "find" him again—that is, have our relationship with him restored—when we turn to him in complete and genuine repentance. He will not allow our sinfulness to permanently disrupt our communion with him.

The other part of the promise, though, is for those who are still seeking God. The implication is that we can find him, but only when we have fully engaged our hearts in the search. It's not enough to treat God as if he is just another item on the buffet table of lifestyle choices. You can't sample a bit of Christianity here and a taste of secular humanism there, wash it all down with a New Age cocktail, and then expect God to take your pursuit very seriously. You need to seek him with the full awareness that this is important stuff; this is the kind of thing that will change your life. God is not interested in a halfhearted flirtation; he wants a complete love relationship with you, one that involves your whole heart.

As he did with the Babylonian exiles, God will draw you back to himself. He promises you will find him if you search in the right way. He sees the whole picture; he knows what is coming up ahead for you. He wants to make sure you are safe and secure with him. But you have to *want* to be with him, and you can prove that by seeking him with all your heart.

———

Lord, I thank you for making yourself accessible to us. I know that if I seek you completely, I will find you; I have no fear that you will withhold your presence from me. Keep me immediately repentant when I sin, so that my relationship with you can be immediately restored.

31

True Confession

If you confess with your mouth, "Jesus is Lord," and believe in your heart that God raised him from the dead, you will be saved.

Romans 10:9

THIS verse presents the most important decision you will make. When you access the promise of salvation, choosing Christ will affect every other decision you face throughout the rest of your life. It will change the way you think, act, speak, and spend your time; it will influence every single day you live and beyond.

The truth is that everyone is a sinner and needs to make the choice to receive salvation. God gives it freely, but only to those who ask for it in the name of the Lord Jesus Christ. The rewards are many, but the ultimate reward is eternal life: living throughout eternity in the presence of God and in full communion with him. Those who have never professed faith in Christ will spend eternity separated from God and from all that is good.

In this verse in Romans, Paul stated two conditions for salvation. The first is that you confess that Jesus is Lord. In a way, that's an odd statement. Isn't it enough to believe that Jesus is Lord? Yes and no;

yes, because you can assume that a believer who is unable to speak will be just as saved as one who is able. No, because Paul was well aware of the persecution a new Christian would face, having experienced it himself. If a person could declare right out loud, in that oppressive environment, that Jesus is Lord—no matter who heard, no matter what the consequences—then that was evidence of genuine faith. The same principle holds true for twenty-first-century believers who openly practice their faith in hostile or oppressive environments—not only in anti-Christian regimes around the world but also in the United States.

Then, too, speaking the Word of God was important among the Jews, who would quietly give voice to the words whenever they meditated on Scripture. They believed that hearing themselves say the truth of Scripture increased their faith. Paul would have grown up believing that, and he no doubt brought that belief with him to his faith in Christ.

The second part of the verse is critical to your understanding of the faith that saves. To believe that Jesus conquered death, that God had the power to raise him from the dead, and that the Resurrection confirmed the truth of Jesus' claims means you know that God and Jesus are who they say they are. To believe in anything less than that is to believe God to be powerless and Jesus dishonest.

That's it. Not much for God to ask of us, in exchange for such a life-altering promise, is it? Considering the outcome, it's not much at all.

———

Lord, thank you for giving the gift of salvation so freely. I confess with my mouth that Jesus is Lord, and I believe God raised him from the dead. I accept your gift of salvation and look forward to spending eternity in loving communion with you.

32

Delighting in the Word

But his delight is in the law of the LORD,
and on his law he meditates day and night.
He is like a tree planted by streams of water,
which yields its fruit in season
and whose leaf does not wither.
Whatever he does prospers.

Psalm 1:2–3

ONE of the dominant characteristics of a person's authentic faith in Christ is the desire—longing, even—to thrive spiritually. What that means may vary with each person and with each passing year in that person's life, but generally it includes growing closer to God, understanding his Word, having an active prayer life, being an effective witness for Christ, and applying biblical truth to everyday living.

This psalm, which also describes the punishment that will come to the wicked, restricts its promises to those people who have that authentic kind of faith, the ones who have placed God in the center of their lives. And while many verses in the Bible promise financial and material prosperity, the two verses from Psalm 1 appear to apply primarily to spiritual prosperity.

The "righteous," as the psalmist referred to believers, were those who continually contemplated "the law of the LORD," which is the extent of the Hebrew Scriptures the writer would have had available to him at the time. They "delighted" in the Law, studying it, memorizing it, teaching it to their children, and most of all, following it—or else the psalmist would not call such a person righteous. The Law would have been deeply ingrained in such a person's life.

The writer compared the righteous to a tree. We get the metaphor right away, but it's unlikely that we have as deep an appreciation for it as the Israelites would have had. Water was—and still is—a precious commodity in that part of the world, and the image of a productive, fruit-bearing, leafy tree meant far more to the Israelites in that day than it ever could to us. This person, this righteous, meditating, God-pleasing person, was prosperous indeed.

One other aspect of the metaphor is where the tree is located—and how it got there. The word "planted" is better translated "transplanted." The tree was placed by the "streams of water," close to the source of that life-giving element. It's not hard to see the writer's point; if we wish to prosper spiritually, we must make sure we are "transplanted" into the kingdom of God and continually draw on the rich, thirst-quenching water that Jesus provides.

Then and only then can we have any hope that we will bear the fruit of the Holy Spirit in our lives—or grasp the promise that we won't wither and die before our time. In other words, then and only then can we have any hope of prospering spiritually.

———

Lord, continually bring your Word to my mind, and give me such a hunger and thirst to know you that I will delight in the opportunity I have to study, memorize, and meditate on the Scriptures.

33

"What Is Truth?"

Then you will know the truth, and the truth will set you free.

John 8:32

I T was Pilate who asked Jesus the ultimate rhetorical question: "What is truth?" (John 18:38) Clearly not interested in either a debate or an answer, a seemingly bored Pilate left the room, announcing to the Jews that he found no fault with Jesus. At the urging of the crowd, he had him scourged anyway. And the rest, of course, is history.

Pilate's question is a valid one, and we should never be so disinterested that we fail to pursue an answer. Truth, as Jesus referred to it in John 8:32, was in part the actual facts about who Jesus was and is and what he accomplished—his messianic role, his atoning work on the cross, his Resurrection, his activity in our lives, and much, much more.

The truth also encompasses Jesus' teachings while he was here on Earth, the teachings of the writers of the canon of Scripture, the ongoing ministry of the Holy Spirit, and the continuing revelation the Spirit brings to us. Embracing the whole truth—and nothing but the truth, of course—is what sets you free. But from what does it free you?

The list is close to endless. Just think of a few ways in which the truth has resulted in freedom in your life. You no longer need to be concerned about life after death, because you know you have eternal life. There is no need for you to spend years in confusion trying to figure out the meaning of life, because Jesus Christ has shown you what life is all about. You are free from the overwhelming power of sin, because the Holy Spirit's ministry includes granting you that release.

You are also free from many things that you may not always sense, depending on where you are in your walk with God, such as loneliness, alienation, lack of direction, condemnation, and a spirit of fear and despair. Yes, those things do plague believers at various times, but every believer has access to both the treatment and the cure, the presence of God in his life.

Try making your own list of things from which Jesus has personally freed you. Mine is a whopper: alcoholism, drug use, smoking, manipulating others, self-destructive behavior, self-righteousness, and—well, that's enough for now. Your list could include a bad habit or an addictive sin, an obsession, religious legalism, a feeling of worthlessness, and a host of negative influences. You may be surprised at how long your list becomes in a very short time. And it's all because you not only recognized the truth when God revealed it to you but also embraced it and took ownership of it for yourself.

———

Lord, thank you for revealing your truth to me—and softening my heart so I was ready to respond to it. Thank you also for setting me free from so many things that once made my life so miserable. Keep me from ever abusing the freedom you have given me.

34

Working for the Good

And we know that in all things God works for the good of those who love him, who have been called according to his purpose.

Romans 8:28

HAVE you ever struggled with this verse? Many have. Even if you haven't personally questioned it, you may know someone who has lashed out in anger toward God, challenging him to show how he could bring good out of the death of a child, the massive loss of life in a terrorist attack, or the unthinkable poverty, starvation, and disease that torture people around the world. It's hard to see any good that could come of such horrendous circumstances.

Part of the problem with this verse stems from faulty translation. The NIV that I've quoted seems to come closest to Paul's original intent. Saying that "God works for the good" is different from stating that "all things work together for the good," which is the idea behind older translations. The NIV implies that despite all the horrible things that happen to people, God continues to work on their behalf. Other translations convey the idea that God orchestrates these catastrophes and then says, "Cheer up! It's all working together for the good!" No wonder some people become angry with him.

Bad things happen to everyone. What should set Christians apart is their unwavering faith in God amid trying circumstances. That isn't always evident, but trials tend to separate those who have truly been "called according to his purpose" from those who allow trials to overwhelm their calling. The faithful know that whether or not they see his activity, God is bringing about good things even as they weep and suffer.

As you look back over your life, you should be able to see something of a plan: if this hadn't happened here, then that wouldn't have happened there; because this other thing *did* happen, all these other things fell into place. If you have been attempting to walk in faithfulness to God, that plan should begin to emerge as something very good. That doesn't mean that everything that happened was good, but it all fit together into a road map of your life that featured some very positive stops along the way to your final destination.

I can clearly see how God's plan shaped my life. I graduated from college during the Vietnam conflict and planned to become an English teacher. Teaching jobs were difficult to come by in the early 1970s, and those that were available often went to male graduates who were trying to avoid military service. At the time, I had no problem with that—far be it from me to think my need for a job was more important than a potential draftee's life—but still, I expected to become a teacher and stay one for the rest of my life. Out of desperation, I took a job at the local newspaper, and through that experience I discovered that my true passion was for journalism. Who knew? I could not have predicted that one, but it all fell into place as that particular chain of events—which didn't appear to me as "good" at the time—unfolded in my life.

As the truth of this promise becomes a reality in your life, make sure you are prepared to help others see it as well. The next time someone speaks against God, thumbing his nose at this verse, you can be the calming and steadying influence that restores his abiding faith in the God who is always on our side, even in the midst of life's terrors.

————

Lord, help me to believe that you are always working on my behalf, with both my temporal good and my eternal good in mind. When the circumstances of life threaten to overwhelm my calling, I trust that you will help me make sure that does not happen.

35

Healing the Land

If my people, who are called by my name, will humble themselves and pray and seek my face and turn from their wicked ways, then will I hear from heaven and will forgive their sin and will heal their land.

2 Chronicles 7:14

I F God answered prayers on the basis of the number of times people uttered a specific prayer, he would indeed forgive and heal our land. For decades, believers have claimed the promise in this verse and urged others to follow the designated steps that would result in national healing. Yet in 2001 the United States experienced the worst terrorist attack in its history. If so many prayed, then why didn't God protect our land? Why hasn't he healed it? The conditions that God established in this verse may hold some clues.

God gave the promise to his people—not to the population as a whole. It's not the unregenerate's responsibility to follow the designated steps. Yet some believers point their fingers at the clueless—people who do not know God and cannot understand the things of God—and expect them to do the praying and repenting. We need to remember that Christians must meet the conditions of the prayer.

God gave a four-step method to obtain his favor on our country. He requires us to humble ourselves, pray, seek his face, and turn from our wicked ways. If this promise has not been fulfilled—and it clearly has not—it's fair to assume we haven't met the conditions. The burden falls to each individual to implement the four steps in his or her own life.

Humbling ourselves requires recognizing God as the almighty Creator and submitting our will to his. It also means that we cannot presume to know what his will is if we have not asked him for that wisdom.

The next two conditions—praying and seeking his face—go hand in hand. Seeking his face requires our time and attention in prayer. We can't say a quick prayer, get on with our day, and expect a holy God to believe we care about our sin as a nation. We need to sit in the presence of the Father, patiently waiting as he reveals his will and his wisdom to us.

Finally, we believers need to turn from our wicked ways. God is concerned about the sin that disables his people. If we hope that God will forgive our country, then *we* must give up the sins that plague our lives.

Do you want to see this promise fulfilled? You can play your part by following the stipulations God set down for his people.

———

Lord, I want to see your blessing come upon our nation. Give me the grace to humble myself before you, seek your face in focused, attentive prayer, and renounce the sins that I confess are still a part of my life.

36

Rest from Labor

There remains, then, a Sabbath-rest for the people of God; for anyone who enters God's rest also rests from his own work, just as God did from his.

Hebrews 4:9–10

I'T'S been decades since we first heard the idea that technology had become so advanced that in no time, Americans would enjoy a typical workweek of thirty hours instead of the usual forty. So certain were the prognosticators that they even suggested that we would face a new challenge—just what to do with all that leisure time.

Most people would probably agree that those predictors were way off the mark. Americans continue to work long hours, and the proliferation of the use of home computers, the Internet, cell phones, and pagers have made time away from work anything but.

Maybe it's happened to you more than you'd like. Friday slips over into Saturday; Monday folds back into Sunday. You remain accessible to those at work even when you're on vacation, and you can't resist the urge to check your e-mails while you're away. To make matters worse, your boss is the human counterpart to the Energizer Bunny: she just keeps going and going and going, and she expects everyone else to do the same.

For God's sake—if not for your own—you need to stop this cycle of constant work. You may not be able to complete your work in five days, but you need to complete it in six. And then take a day off, a full day with no work, no planning for work, no obsessing over work, no catching up on work-related e-mails or other correspondence—nothing at all.

If you want to get radical, return to the old biblical ideal of the Sabbath-rest—which was the norm, not a fanatical departure from the norm, until forty years ago when "blue laws" forbidding Sunday selling began to be repealed. Be prepared for a battle, though, because with few exceptions, our 24/7 culture considers keeping the Sabbath a quaint and obsolete tradition. The writer of Hebrews seems to have anticipated that; he encouraged believers to "make every effort to enter" into the Sabbath-rest (Heb. 4:11). It's ironic, but you have to fight these days for the day of rest you're entitled to take.

One thing we seem to forget is that our day of rest was a part of creation and not just a day tagged on to the other six as an afterthought. God never intended it to be a day of rigorous duty and obligation. He wants us to enjoy it as a time of recharging and restoring our strength and energy. The promise is that a Sabbath-rest "remains"—we have only to practice it.

———

Lord, I know I've been working too long and too hard. I know you gave me the Sabbath for my benefit, but it's so hard for me to see how I can take off an entire day each week. Give me the grace and the discipline to stop the cycle of constant work and truly learn to enter into your Sabbath-rest.

37

Prophets of Integrity

And afterward,
I will pour out my Spirit on all people.
Your sons and daughters will prophesy,
your old men will dream dreams,
your young men will see visions.

Joel 2:28

ANY have written and spoken in recent years about the role of visionaries in the church, primarily because more and more people have set themselves up as prophets of God. While most would agree that the function of a prophet is still valid and a fulfillment of this promise given in Joel, false pronouncements have caused us to question many of the messages people make in the name of God.

It's important to understand that prophets not only prophesy about the future but also provide commentary from God on the current state of the church and society—usually, not-so-pleasant commentary. A prophet tells it as God sees it, without any fear of the repercussions. People have been known to kill the messenger, and prophets are well aware of that.

Anyone can call himself or herself a prophet, establish a ministry, and take a full roster of conferences on the road. You should never fear testing what such a person says and teaches.

How can you know if a person is truly a prophet of God? The first test you should apply—as with everything in life—is whether or not the prophet's teachings line up with Scripture. Second, the prophet should be a person of unquestioned integrity, with humility right at the top of the list of essential characteristics; a prophet can speak forcefully and confidently without being arrogant and prideful. Finally—and this falls under the integrity category but warrants special mention—a true prophet does not prophesy for a price. Valid ministry support is one thing; prophecy for profit is another.

But what about dreams and visions? How can you know if they are a fulfillment of God's promise of spiritual blessing, a projection of your own hopes and fears, or evidence of demonic activity? This is where discernment is critical. If you have been experiencing dreams and visions and you are having trouble sorting them out, it's essential that you share your experiences with a respected and trustworthy person who is clearly gifted in this area—a pastor or a spiritual director, for instance.

Realize, too, what must precede this kind of outpouring of the Spirit. The promise was given after the Lord called the Israelites to repentance: "Turn to me with all your heart, with fasting, with weeping and with mourning" (Joel 2:12). The prophet continued with a call for a sacred assembly of all the people during which the priests would weep and plead with God on their behalf. God would reward their repentance with blessing and protection from their enemies. And then, the spiritual blessing would come.

Even though you must be careful when it comes to spiritual activities such as prophecies, dreams, and visions, there's no question that such activity can be from God. He promised that an outpouring of his Spirit would result in unusual spiritual blessing—and the vessels of that blessing would cross both age and gender barriers. Always remain open to the possibility that God might be revealing things to you in an unusual way.

———

Lord, help me to discern what is from you and what is not. Let me find that healthy middle ground between skepticism and naivete. Thank you for pouring out your blessing on us.

38

Infinite Patience

The Lord is not slow in keeping his promise, as some understand slowness. He is patient with you, not wanting anyone to perish, but everyone to come to repentance.

2 Peter 3:9

HAVE you ever wondered why God has taken so long to bring his kingdom to pass? The New Testament writers expressed such a sense of urgency about the return of Jesus Christ, but here we are, two millennia later, and he clearly has not returned. The verse immediately preceding this one in 2 Peter offers an explanation: "But do not forget this one thing, dear friends: With the Lord a day is like a thousand years, and a thousand years are like a day." To God, who of course exists outside of time, it's been only a moment since Jesus' ascension.

Peter was making the point that God is exceedingly patient with his creation; in essence, he is promising not to lose his patience with us. Yes, he will fulfill his promise to usher in the kingdom of God. Yes, Jesus Christ will return. Yes, there will come a time devoid of suffering, pain, sorrow, and tears. But in the meantime, God is waiting, taking his time, giving as many people as possible the opportunity to accept the free gift of salvation that he has so graciously offered.

Think of everything God has to put up with as he waits. People ignore him, mock him, blaspheme his name, rebel against him, disobey him, and reject him. His own people often treat him with disrespect. And yet he waits, withholding his judgment and punishment so more people can take advantage of his offer of eternal life.

Likewise, he withholds his ultimate blessing—the return of Jesus Christ—so more believers can repent of their continued sin. He has a truly amazing capacity for both patience and grace, lavishing both on us as if we deserved it. We don't, but that's the way God is, always giving us what we don't deserve.

Even though he is the very definition of infinite patience, God has always given his people a driving desire to see their loved ones come to Christ. He wants us to make the most of our time on Earth by sharing the gospel with as many people as we can. We don't know when God will bestow his ultimate blessing on us, and that's the way he wants it. What we do in the meantime should make all the difference in the world.

————

Lord, remind me of your patience when I start to get anxious that I will never see your promises come to pass. Thank you for delaying the return of Christ until I had accepted your offer of eternal life. And when it comes to concern for my unsaved friends, grant me that same sense of urgency in sharing Christ with them that the New Testament writers expressed.

39

Supernatural Strength

I can do everything through him who gives me strength.

Philippians 4:13

Y OU'VE no doubt heard stories of people who found superhuman strength in times of duress—when a person is trapped under a car, for instance, and some petite young woman comes along and lifts the car up just enough to free the victim. You've got to believe that God is in some way involved in a dramatic rescue like that. Maybe our heroine was silently reciting this verse, or maybe God just wanted the victim to live.

But far more numerous are the everyday heroes who stand on the promise implied in this verse, people who do superhuman things like work in a pediatric hospice center, apply salve to the sores of AIDS victims, or clean up after a homeless alcoholic who has just lost the meal served to him at the soup kitchen. You've got to believe that God is in every way involved in dramatic rescues like those as well.

Paul's intention in writing the words of this verse to the Philippians was not to boast of any special relationship with the Lord. He meant to encourage the Philippian church to draw on the strength and power that the Lord promises to his followers (Rom. 16:25). He was saying, "I have been empowered by Christ; you can be empowered by Christ, too."

How does Christ strengthen you? Perhaps there is something in your life right now that is exceedingly difficult but that you have somehow found the strength to deal with. Maybe your father is terminally ill or your daughter just had an abortion; your son is stationed in a war-torn country; your job is on the line; your best friend has bitterly betrayed you; your doctor has just informed you that you need surgery. Or maybe your difficulty is something good that you feel ill equipped to handle, like preaching the sermon next Sunday while the pastor is out of town or heading up a significant project at work. It's Christ who empowers you to do those things.

Keep this in mind: God is not promising that you will be able to accomplish things outside the realm of human possibility. He may choose to work that way, of course, but that's not the intent of this verse. He also is not promising that you will be able to do things that are outside of his will ("I can make that woman fall in love with me through Christ who strengthens me!"). What he *is* promising is that he will strengthen and empower his people to accomplish what he asks them to do and withstand the pressures and attacks that come against them.

God's promises are not magic tricks. They are the gifts a loving Father gives to his children, powerful gifts that we must use responsibly.

———

Lord, thank you for making so many things possible in my life. Help me to keep this verse in mind when circumstances stretch and challenge me, as well as when I face trials and other difficulties in life. Let me never forget to draw on your strength instead of trying to depend on my own.

40

Muttering Your Meditation

Do not let this Book of the Law depart from your mouth; meditate on it day and night, so that you may be careful to do everything written in it. Then you will be prosperous and successful.

Joshua 1:8

HAVE you ever wondered what the first part of this verse means? It sounds as if God was requiring Joshua to walk around speaking nothing but the words of the Book of the Law. If so, that doesn't bode well for the rest of us.

Not surprisingly, that's not what God meant. That part of the command referred to the way the ancient Israelites, as well as people from other cultures, performed the practice of meditation. They literally muttered the passage they were meditating on, out of a belief that hearing one's own voice speaking the passage helped them remember and gain wisdom from it.

That's good advice for us today. We've grown up with the words of our elementary school teachers ringing in our heads. They warned us not to sound out the words as we read to ourselves, because they considered it a bad habit. But we're adults now, and it may be time to return to the ancients' method of meditation. (Monks have known the value of this method for centuries, but how many of us have the opportunity to learn from them? Maybe we need to make the opportunity!)

Whatever method of meditation you choose to use—whether you "mutter" the words, silently think on them, or repeat a passage of Scripture over and over again in your head—it remains a valid practice for you today. Meditating on the Word of God makes it sink deep into your spirit so that you may "be careful to do everything written in it." In other words, it becomes such an intrinsic part of your life that you begin automatically to think about Scripture when a difficult choice or a sticky situation confronts you.

Note also that prosperity and success depend on being careful to do "everything" in the Word. That's not meant to be taken literally, of course; the point God is making is that our freedom does not include the option to pick and choose which portions of Scripture we decide to obey. Partial obedience, as God made clear throughout his dealings with Israel, is not godly obedience.

In this promise is your formula for success and prosperity: a constant attentiveness to the Word of God plus obedience to its teachings. It's a formula that has proven to work time and time again.

———

Lord, give me such a love for your Word that I will want to meditate on it day and night. I pray that your Word will become so deeply embedded in my spirit that I never be at a loss for your wisdom when I face difficulties. Thank you for linking spiritual riches with a practice that has such profound temporal and eternal benefits.

41

Already Clean

You are already clean because of the word I have spoken to you.

John 15:3

THIS assurance, which Jesus delivered in the midst of his discourse on the vine and the vinedresser, seems almost out of place. Why was Jesus talking about cleansing in the context of pruning the branches from the vines? Though you could probably make a connection there, what's important to remember is that this section of Scripture records the words Jesus spoke during the event we call the Last Supper.

Earlier in the evening, as he began washing the feet of his disciples, Jesus answered Peter's objection with these words: "Unless I wash you, you have no part with me" (John 13:8). He then explained the need for washing, both as a one-time cleansing at the moment of salvation and an ongoing "bathing" as part of the process of sanctification. In John 15:3, Jesus reminded the disciples that they were already clean—not because he had just washed their feet, but because they had embraced his teachings.

The Word of God has the power to keep us continually cleansed, as we allow the Holy Spirit to convict us when we disobey what God has so clearly presented in the Scriptures. Because we know the Word—in order to receive salvation we had to accept the truth of the gospel—we are without excuse. To remain in the filthiness and squalor of sin is to deny the Word; to be clean is to embrace the Word and allow it to do its purifying work in our lives.

Think about that the next time you're really muddy, sweaty, or dusty. You know how great a shower feels when you've gotten yourself good and grimy? That's nothing compared to how great it can feel to have the Word of God cleanse you when you repent after being swallowed in a sinkhole of sin. There's just nothing like it. No shower gel on the market—regardless of its aromatic or therapeutic benefits—can possibly compare to the deep-down cleansing power of the Bible.

If you truly want to serve God, you need to see yourself as a vessel through which he works in the world. And you need to make sure that you always present yourself as a clean vessel, one that will not pollute the ministry he seeks to accomplish through you.

You are already clean and saved—that is Jesus' promise to you—so now keep yourself clean and sanctified by welcoming the Holy Spirit's ministry of conviction in your life. When you do, you can rightfully claim your place among the pure and holy vessels that God has set aside for his service.

————

Lord, I want to be clean in your sight. Give me the grace always to be open to the convicting ministry of the Holy Spirit, so that I may immediately turn from the sin that the Spirit reveals to me and you may place me back in your service. Thank you for your ongoing work of purification in my life.

42

Comfort for the Afflicted

Shout for joy, O heavens;
rejoice, O earth;
burst into song, O mountains!
For the LORD comforts his people
and will have compassion on his afflicted ones.

Isaiah 49:13

F OR some time, Bible students believed that ancient Middle East-
erners used to collect their tears in small bottles fashioned from
animal skins. Scholars disproved that notion, but it's a romantic idea
anyway—imagine having your own private collection of tears! Then
there could be no doubt who had suffered the most among your circle of friends. Another myth was that mourners collected their tears
in bottles and buried them with the deceased person. The bigger the
bottle, the greater the suffering of the living—or the greater the
stature of the dead, depending on which story you believe.

Apparently, those fanciful ideas stemmed from a combination of
factors: David's reference to God putting the psalmist's tears "into
[his] bottle" in Psalm 56:8 (NKJV), and the tear-shaped perfume bottles sometimes found in the coffins of ancient Israelites—often the

only material possession the Israelites ever buried with a body. It's unclear what David meant—maybe those scholars are wrong after all—but the important thing is that God does "save" our tears in some manner. In other words, he has a record of all the sorrows and losses and afflictions that have caused us to mourn and grieve and shed collectable tears.

Sometimes when we're striving to cope with a significant loss, especially the senseless death of a loved one, we try to make sense out of it. We look for God's purpose: Why did he take this person at this time? What possible reason could he have for allowing that person to suffer in that way? Our reason begins to interfere with the consolation God is extending to us. The heavens and the earth and the mountains see how God is comforting us, and they "shout . . . rejoice . . . burst into song" over the wonderful way God shows compassion to his people. And there we are, questioning, reasoning, engaging our minds at a time when our hearts need to be most fully open to his presence.

We will all suffer pain throughout the course of our lives. But Jesus, the "Man of sorrows," has "borne our griefs and carried our sorrows" (Isa. 53:3, 4 NKJV). God knows every loss we have suffered, every pain we have endured, every distressful situation that has saddened us. Paul describes how God not only comforts us but also gives us the grace to comfort others:

Praise be to the God and Father of our Lord Jesus Christ, the Father of compassion and the God of all comfort, who comforts us in all our troubles, so that we can comfort those in any trouble with the comfort we ourselves have received from God. For just as the sufferings of Christ flow over into our lives, so also through Christ our comfort overflows. If we are distressed, it is for your comfort and salvation; if we are comforted, it is for your comfort, which produces in you patient endurance of the same sufferings we suffer. And our hope for you is firm, because we know that just as you share in our sufferings, so also you share in our comfort. (2 Cor. 1:3–7)

God promises to continue to bear our griefs and soothe our sorrows until the day comes when there will be no more need for tears. The heavens and earth and mountains seem to be able to see that day better than we can.

———

Lord, I don't understand why you have allowed certain things to happen in my life. It's enough for me to know that your promise of comfort will remain with me all the days that I live. Keep me open to your comforting presence and keep me from trying to reason with those things that only you can comprehend.

43

Full to Overflowing

Honor the LORD with your wealth,
with the firstfruits of all your crops;
then your barns will be filled to overflowing,
and your vats will brim over with new wine.

Proverbs 3:9–10

ARE your barns filled to overflowing? Are your vats brimming over with new wine? Probably not. We've moved so far from an agriculture-based society that many biblical images fall flat with us. Most of us don't have any gardens to begin with, so honoring God with the firstfruits of all our "crops" becomes a bit of a challenge.

But most of us do have income and possessions. Honoring God with our firstfruits, then, translates into giving of our income and using our possessions wisely. The translated promise means we will receive more than we need in return.

For some people, tithing—giving 10 percent of their income to God—is a difficult concept to understand. They live from one paycheck to the next, never able to get ahead, unexpected car repairs or medical bills swallowing their meager savings. For other people, certain churches' and ministries' abuses in handling money have soured them on giving any more funds to so-called representatives of God. Still others have never received adequate teaching on tithing. And some people are just plain selfish, choosing to use all their wealth for their own enjoyment and never caring about the crushing spiritual and physical burdens that their money could help alleviate.

God has a suggestion for all those who question or object to the practice of tithing: "'Bring the whole tithe into the storehouse, that there may be food in my house. Test me in this,' says the LORD Almighty, 'and see if I will not throw open the floodgates of heaven and pour out so much blessing that you will not have room enough for it'" (Mal. 3:10). Sounds a lot like the fulfillment of the promise in Proverbs 3:9–10, doesn't it: barns overflowing, vats brimming over, more than you can contain.

Perhaps you've long been a giver to God but never a tither. Ten percent looks like a lot to you; it represents money that could go toward the rising cost of living, better-quality clothes that would last longer, or your children's college education funds, so they won't have to scrimp on everything the way you've had to. God wants you to put him to the test. He sees your need, he sees your lack, and he wants to bless you.

In giving, you will receive. That's one of the immutable laws of the kingdom of God. It's one of the many paradoxes and promises that characterize God's way of doing things. And it's one of the concepts that most baffles the world. But once you've put God to the test, you will no longer be baffled. Instead, you will be blessed.

––––––––

Lord, give me the faith to believe this promise. I want to help others, but I also want to provide for my own family. As I give to you, I trust that you will not allow my family to suffer.

44

He Will Do What He Says

For no matter how many promises God has made, they are "Yes" in Christ. And so through him the "Amen" is spoken by us to the glory of God.

2 Corinthians 1:20

No two biblical scholars seem to agree on how many promises God has made. Estimates range from about seven thousand obvious promises to thirty thousand—roughly the total number of verses in the Bible. Interpreting what is a promise is apparently a highly subjective enterprise.

But this much we do know: if God said he would do it, then he will do it. The writer of Numbers recorded this reminder that the Lord gave through Balaam: "God is not a man, that he should lie, or a son of man, that he should change his mind" (23:19). God is not at all like us. He is honest and trustworthy and faithful. Always.

As Paul expressed in this verse, God's promises are "Yes" and "Amen" in Christ. That's as good as an oath, a vow that God takes very seriously. God vows that he will make good on all his promises—and he reminds us that all of his promises find their fulfillment in his Son, Jesus Christ.

Everyone has moments of doubting certain of God's promises. If a chronic illness has debilitated you, it's hard to continue to believe God's promises for healing, day in and day out of unrelenting pain. If you've been living on the edge financially for decades, it's hard to continue to believe his promises for prosperity. But our moments of doubting in no way affect the validity of the guarantees God has made.

Think of all the areas of your life that God's promises affect: family, finances, physical well-being, personal security, relationships, faith and spirituality, job and career, and so much more. Don't let one not-yet-fulfilled promise blind you to the many that God has made good on. If you were to list even the lower total of biblical promises, you would discover that God has delivered on most of them in your life if you are a member of his family.

The incarnate "Amen" fulfilled every one of God's promises when he went to the cross for us. Just as he dealt with all of our sins—past, present, and future—in his sacrificial act, so all of the promises of God—past, present, and future—found their completion in that act. He is the embodiment of all that God has said; he is the living representation of the vow made by the living God. He is the permanent proof that God keeps his promises.

————

Lord, I am so grateful to you that you make good on your promises—whether I believe them or not. Lord, I do believe; I just need a little help with my unbelief. You have never given me any reason to doubt you. Forgive me when I begin to wonder if what you have said will really come to pass.

45

The Lord Will Provide

And my God will meet all your needs according to his glorious riches in Christ Jesus.

Philippians 4:19

IN many churches across the country, believers regularly sing a praise song called "Jehovah-Jireh, My Provider." Its lyrics include the words of this verse and those of several other Bible verses, mainly from the New Testament. But *Jehovah-Jireh,* one of the many Hebrew phrases Christians use to describe the activity of God in their lives, has a decidedly Old Testament origin. It was the name of a place where God met the needs of two people in a mighty and miraculous way.

Abraham, his son Isaac, and two servants had traveled to Mount Moriah to make a sacrifice to God. Telling the servants to stay behind, Abraham took Isaac to a designated spot on the mountain. On the way there, Isaac understandably asked where Abraham expected to find a lamb for the sacrifice. Answering simply, "God will provide," Abraham began to build an altar. Imagine Isaac's shock when

Abraham told him to lie down on the altar—Abraham's beloved son was to be the sacrifice!

But then, in one of the most dramatic scenes in all of Scripture, just as Abraham was about to slay his son, God called from heaven: "Do not lay a hand on the boy. . . . Now I know that you fear God, because you have not withheld from me your son, your only son" (Gen. 22:12). In the nick of time, God saved the day, Isaac's life, and Abraham's grief.

You probably know the rest of the story: a ram, miraculously caught in a thicket, appeared out of nowhere, and Abraham offered it as a sacrifice in place of Isaac. And Abraham did one more thing: he named the place of sacrifice "The LORD Will Provide" (Gen. 22:14). In ancient Hebrew culture, to name a thing was to take possession of it; on Mount Moriah Abraham took possession of God's provision, both on that day and in the days to come.

When you begin to doubt God's provision, think about Abraham and Isaac on Mount Moriah. The God who intervened and provided an alternate sacrifice to spare Isaac's life can certainly supply your needs. No need is too small or too big for God to meet.

Remember, though, that this promise applies to your genuine needs, not your wants. Think you need a wide-screen television? God may think otherwise. But he may think—or rather, know—that you really need peace of mind, a reliable car, and a faithful friend. He also knows what you will need in the future. No need to be concerned. All he has to do is dip his hand into the riches he has stored up for you in glory, and it's as good as done.

———

Lord, you have already met so many of my needs. I know I can trust you to meet all of the others. Never let me forget the lesson that Abraham learned, that you are the Lord who will provide everything: the big, the small, and the in-between.

46

Supernatural Teacher

But the Counselor, the Holy Spirit, whom the Father will send in my name, will teach you all things and will remind you of everything I have said to you.

John 14:26

IF you've ever wondered how on earth the writers of the Bible remembered all that God wanted put down in Scripture, you have your answer here. God sent the Holy Spirit to continue the teaching ministry of Jesus and to help the disciples recall what the Lord had already taught them. To a group of men who often failed to understand what Jesus had just said to them, this had to come as welcome news indeed.

The Holy Spirit operates in much the same way in your life today. Any time you've suddenly remembered a Scripture that is helpful in your immediate situation, you can thank the Holy Spirit for bringing it to mind. When you're undecided about a particular choice you have to make, the Holy Spirit is there to instruct you and guide you into making the right decision.

Most of all, you can count on the Holy Spirit to reveal to you the truth of Scripture. Like the disciples, believers today don't always fully comprehend what Jesus taught when he was on earth, or what God has been telling his people from the very beginning. Your knowledge and understanding of the Scriptures is a gradually unfolding process. What you understood on one level two years ago, you may need to understand on a much deeper level today. The Holy Spirit is the one who sorts all that out for you and makes it intelligible, using words and images that are particularly meaningful to you. He is your personal tutor in the ways and the truths of God.

The Holy Spirit also actively participates in our worship each time we take Communion, a ritual that calls to mind everything that Jesus accomplished on the cross on our behalf. As we hear the words of the ritual and partake symbolically of Jesus' body and blood, the Holy Spirit reminds us in wordless ways of the awesome sacrifice God made in allowing his beloved only Son to die for us.

While Jesus was still on earth, he assured his disciples that God the Father would send a Counselor who would come alongside them and minister in his name. God fulfilled that part of John 14:26 two thousand years ago. He fulfilled the rest of the verse both then *and* in all the intervening years, as the Holy Spirit instructed believers down through the centuries. His ministry of instruction is still active and accessible—and Jesus' promise still stands.

———

Lord, thank you for sending the Holy Spirit to reveal your truth to me. I know I can rely on him to lead me into all truth, to instruct me as he sees fit.

47

Eternal Trophy

Do not be afraid of what you are about to suffer. I tell you, the devil will put some of you in prison to test you, and you will suffer persecution for ten days. Be faithful, even to the point of death, and I will give you the crown of life.

Revelation 2:10

L IKE much of the Book of Revelation, the second sentence in this verse is the subject of endless debate. But no one disputes the meanings of the sentences that flank the middle one: Christians will suffer persecution, but they have no reason to fear. If they remain faithful—even if it means their deaths—God will give them the crown of life.

When we hear the word *crown,* we may automatically think of royalty. But the believers in the city of Smyrna, to whom Jesus addressed this portion of Revelation, had a different frame of reference. To them, a crown represented victory, a kind of trophy winners of athletic competitions received and people who had distinguished themselves by their service to the community earned.

Given that, they would have clearly understood what the Lord was promising to them: the crown of eternal life, a trophy for their victory over persecution and death and for their faithful service to God in life. Some Bible scholars also believe that the crown may represent a special reward in heaven for those who die a martyr's death.

For those of us who live in a culture in which persecution—if we can even call it that—is limited to comparatively insignificant emotional, psychological, and political harassment, the image of the crown of life symbolizes something far different from what it means to, say, Muslim converts to Christianity who continue to live in Islamic countries. Those believers face the daily possibility that the promise of the crown of life to those martyred for their faith will be fulfilled in their own lives.

Likewise, missionaries such as Martin and Gracia Burnham, whom extremists in the Philippines held captive in 2001, received their crowns as they continued in faithful service to God to the point of death for Martin. Serving God on the mission field carries risks that few of us back home can comprehend; many missionaries live with the constant threat that this could be the day their persecutors give them an opportunity to receive their trophies.

The same principle holds true for twenty-first-century believers who openly practice their faith in hostile or oppressive environments around the world. Christmas, it seems, is a particularly tough time to be a Christian in some areas; in December 2002 alone, Muslim extremists killed three young girls in a grenade attack on a Pakistani church; in Vietnam, four small children and three unborn babies died after police released an unknown gas in a Christian church during a worship service. Also in Vietnam, three pastors were killed by lethal injection after being imprisoned for practicing their faith. Sudan, Indonesia, and a host of other countries are hotbeds of persecution against Christians. Ministries such as International Christian Concern and Voice of the Martyrs, among others, do their best to make the world aware of these atrocities; unfortunately, unless an attack is an openly public one like the Burnhams', few people hear of the modern-day martyrs who have lost their lives because of their faith in Christ.

We may—thankfully—never know what it's like to suffer real persecution for our faith, but those who do will receive their reward from one who knows all too well what it's like. Jesus suffered the ultimate version. He assures us that our suffering is only temporary and that physical death is not the end to life. He will personally grant the crown of life to those who remain faithful.

———

Lord, I lift up those believers who are undergoing persecution throughout the world today. I ask that you give them the grace and the power to remain faithful to the end, that they may receive a special reward directly from your compassionate hand.

48

A "More Full" Life

The thief comes only to steal and kill and destroy; I have come that they may have life, and have it to the full.

John 10:10

PEOPLE who have been "churched" for any time at all have probably heard the phrase "the abundant life" kicked around a lot. Believers use it mostly in the context of this verse, in which Jesus compared the life he gives to the kind of existence the Pharisees (the "thief") offered, an existence of loss and death. By comparison, of course, the abundant life looks promising indeed.

But just what was Jesus promising in this verse? What exactly does it mean to have life "to the full"? And why can't we seem to experience it?

In one sense, all believers are already living the abundant life, whether or not life looks or feels that way to us. We've been spared the agony of an eternity separated from the love of God. We have the Holy Spirit to guide, comfort, and enlighten us—and to convict us of sin, so we might repent and get back to the abundant life God intends us to live. And we have at least the potential of experiencing a full life within a community of faith, with like-minded believers with whom we share a sense of mission and system of support.

Not enough? God offers more, as usual—and literally, it seems. Some versions render the phrase in this verse as "more abundant" or even "more full." God didn't stop at mere abundance or fullness. He wants us to know that we can live a life of "more"—more of everything he has promised us in his Word. And since his promises cover the gamut of life, from material prosperity to physical health to spiritual riches to emotional well-being, we have reason to believe that we can see his promises fulfilled to the max. To fail to believe in his guarantees is to give the thieves a measure of victory, as they continue to harass us with their message of destruction.

When we come to believe in God, Jesus restores life to us initially; we were dead in our sins, and through his precious offer of salvation, he breathes life back into our dying selves. He restores to us all that is good in life, and then he goes a step further. His promise states that he returns to us the possibility of experiencing all that is *great* in life, all the blessings that flow from the generous hand of the Father. And that's more than we could ever ask for or even imagine.

———

Lord, I know I could be living life more abundantly, because you have promised that I could. Help me to experience that "more full" life by daily seeking more of you, believing that you want me to receive every blessing, every gift, every reward you have for me. Thank you for offering so much to me.

49

The Spoils of War

No, in all these things we are more than conquerors through him who loved us.

Romans 8:37

F OR a writer who at other times exhibited a tremendous amount of passion, Paul was surprisingly reserved in this most triumphant verse. We aren't mere conquerors, he told us, we're *more* than conquerors! We should see exclamation marks all over the place!

Especially when you consider what "all these things" refers to: trouble, hardship, persecution, famine, nakedness, danger, the sword. Oh, and facing death all day long, since our tormenters see us as sheep to be slaughtered (Rom. 7:35–36). And yet, Paul simply reminded us that the one who loves us has given us the victory— and then some—over all those things.

Maybe Paul had become so accustomed to the astonishing ways of God that it was natural for him to see us as more than conquerors. Jesus had already conquered the principalities and powers of this world through his death on the cross, and thus proved himself—and us, through his life in us—to be invincible. Jesus' resurrection assures victory over Paul's laundry list of "things."

So what has this victory cost us? Not a thing worth holding on to, including our physical bodies; even in death we lose nothing and gain everything. Instead of suffering losses, we get to march triumphantly, bearing the spoils of the battle Jesus fought. We get things like eternal life, eternal love, and the eternal presence of God.

And that's how Paul could call us more than conquerors. Someone else paid the ultimate price for us, and all we have to do is ride into town on his coattails and gather up the wealth and riches that once belonged to the enemy. Jesus stands before us in his grace and mercy and opens wide his battle-scarred arms. "Here," he says with a tender, compassionate smile. "This is all yours, the treasures that I unlocked as I hung on the cross."

It's his love that did all this, you know. Jesus handed over not only the spoils of war but also the victory itself. We have no need to fear the enemy because Jesus settled the enemy's fate once and for all. In the process, he made us superconquerors, more than overcomers, simply by our association with himself. And if there's one thing you can be sure of when it comes to superconquerors, they—we—can never be defeated.

———

Thank you, Lord, for suffering the scars of battle on my behalf. You have given me all the riches you acquired in that ultimate struggle, and you freed me from the fear of my enemies, as well as the fear of death. Thank you for making me more than a conqueror—in fact, a superconqueror—through your overwhelming love.

50

Deliverance from Trouble

The righteous cry out, and the LORD hears them;
he delivers them from all their troubles.

Psalm 34:17

NOT feeling very righteous these days? Think this verse doesn't apply to you as a result? Take heart. It does. It's our New Testament understanding of the word "righteous" that's got you hung up. We're in the habit of thinking of the righteousness—the sinlessness and moral perfection—of Christ. But that's not what the Israelites understood the term to mean.

To the Israelites, a righteous person was one who did the right things under the circumstances in which he found himself. A righteous person was not one without faults. If you are relying on God for strength, guidance, and victory over sin, you are a righteous person. So go ahead and cry out! The Lord will hear you.

Not only that, he will also deliver you. You don't have to go through all kinds of God-pleasing religious rituals to find the immediate release and relief you need. Your "crying out" implies an emergency situation in which you realize that you have no hope of any kind except from the Lord. That's what God wanted you to see all along: you have no rescuer apart from him. Even if your deliverance comes through human means, it is God who directed and empowered others to come to your assistance.

God loves to see a humble heart in his children. As long as we shut him out and think we can handle the problems of life on our own, his abundant promises will not be activated for us. How can we expect him to deliver us if we treat him as if he is of no consequence in our lives? We can't. But when we cry out to him in humility and helplessness, he is quick to respond.

What are the troubles in your life today? We all have them; some of us are just more inclined to admit it than others are. God wants you to go to him with your afflictions, to expose the sorrows in your heart, and to give voice to them. Cry, shout, scream, sob—it makes no difference to him. He will hear you, and he will pull you out of your despair and place his peace within you.

Don't try to find relief from your problems anywhere else. It just won't work. The rest God offers is incomparable. He doesn't want you to suffer any delay in receiving that relief by holding your troubles inside. Let them out. Let the only one who can deliver you hear your cry. He's waiting.

———

Lord, I've been guilty of thinking I could manage life's difficulties myself, and I've been wrong. You are my only source for hope and help. As I come up against the troubles of life, keep me in an attitude of humility and helplessness until I remember to cry out to you for deliverance.

51

Glory after Death

Then the righteous will shine like the sun in the kingdom of their Father. He who has ears, let him hear.

Matthew 13:43

To fully appreciate this promise, look at the verses preceding it. Jesus had just explained the parable of the weeds to his disciples. That was the parable in which a man's enemy stole into his field and sowed weeds among the good seed. The man advised his workers not to pull the weeds but to let them grow along with the wheat; at the harvest, his workers would burn the weeds and take the wheat into the man's barn.

The disciples needed an explanation even though they had ears to hear. The sower, Jesus said, was the Son of Man—himself, of course. The good seed represented believers; the weeds, unbelievers; the enemy, the devil; the harvest, the end of the age. At the harvest, the angels will weed out those who do evil and throw them into the fire. And then we come to the promise: the believers, whose righteousness the prevalence of sin in the world has obscured, will shine like the sun in the kingdom of God the Father.

That's what our glorious future looks like. Death, which seems always to be depicted amid an atmosphere of doom and gloom, will not be shrouded in darkness for us. Instead, we will experience honor as we are brought before the throne of God, reflecting his brilliance, his radiance, his glory.

It's hard to imagine, isn't it? We can't even look directly at the sun when it's at its brightest, and yet we will somehow become like the sun. We will be brought into God's "barn"—his kingdom—having escaped the fiery end that will come to some of those we knew. And all the while, we will be very much aware of how close we came to meeting that same punishment, had we not had ears to hear the gospel of Christ and respond to it.

It's only by the grace of God that he can consider any of us good seed. Much of the time, we feel more like pesky weeds than beneficial wheat. We just hope and pray that God's angels will be able to distinguish us from the real weeds.

And of course they will. They will see the unmistakable hand of the Sower on us, and they will usher us into the kingdom—where somehow God will cause us to shine like the sun.

Lord, thank you for promising to rescue me from the fire that I surely deserve. Let me continue to have ears that hear what you are saying to me, so that I may walk in obedience to you until that glorious day of harvest.

52

A God Who Hears

Then you will call upon me and come and pray to me, and I will listen to you.

Jeremiah 29:12

THIS promise is one that God made at a specific time to a specific group of people, and he fulfilled it as promised. But the underlying principle—that our God is a God who hears our prayers—is every bit as relevant to us today.

The historical situation once again involved the Jews whom King Nebuchadnezzar had taken from Jerusalem and held in captivity in Babylon. The prophet Jeremiah warned them not to listen to the false prophets who were predicting their immediate release, but to listen to God, who was telling them that their captivity would last seventy years. At the end of that seventy-year period, Jeremiah told the captives, the people's hearts would be turned back toward God. They would call on him and pray to him, and he would hear.

Seventy years later, Daniel, representing the people of Israel, began fasting and approached God in sackcloth and ashes—and no, that's not just an expression. Penitent Jews really did put on scratchy sackcloth garments and rubbed ashes on themselves to symbolize both their affliction and sincerity before God. Daniel's prayer of repentance on behalf of the captives apparently did catch God's ear, because Daniel immediately received a divine visitation in which God showed the events that were to come (see Daniel 9).

The promise for us, in this day and in this place, has to do with God's desire to receive our prayers. We want so much to hear from him that we often overlook the fact that he wants to hear from us. He's the one who prompts us to pray—would any of us pray if he didn't?—and he promises to hear us when we do.

To those in Daniel and Jeremiah's time, this was especially meaningful, surrounded as they were by nations whose gods were deaf and dumb structures made of metal and clay. Our idols—money, leisure, celebrity, and so forth—may be less apparent, but they are no less real. As in the time of the Babylonian captivity, our idols can neither move us to pray nor hear our prayers. God does both.

Whenever you are tempted to think that God is not listening to you, remember this verse and the promise it contains.

———

Lord, you are the one prompting me to pray right now; I could not and would not pray were it not for your gentle reminders. Let me never doubt your ability and willingness to hear what I say in prayer to you. Thank you for wanting to hear from me even more than I want to hear from you.

53

Great Is His Faithfulness

God, who has called you into fellowship with his Son Jesus Christ our Lord, is faithful.

1 Corinthians 1:9

HAVE you ever stopped to consider just how extensive God's faithfulness is? As a believer, you probably feel assured of his steadfastness. But his faithfulness extends far beyond his relationship with those who have turned to him in faith. He is equally faithful to those who have yet to meet him, as he is continually calling to them, beckoning them to enter in to a personal relationship with him through his Son, Jesus Christ.

That's how everyone comes to Jesus—through the initial call of God. Think of how faithful he was to you before you placed your trust in him. He never gave up on you. He kept calling to you, sometimes in whispers, sometimes in silence, and perhaps, sometimes in the shout of devastating circumstances. He wanted you to turn to him so he could pull you out of the life you were living and give you new life in Christ.

My own journey of faith exemplifies this. As a child, I responded to the gospel message but didn't understand the implications of a complete surrender to the lordship of Christ. I walked away from church—and God—at the age of twelve, and for the next ten years, I ignored or failed to recognize his many overtures toward me. Looking back on that time, I can now see that he beckoned me to return to him through the prayers and witness of the few Christians I knew, the tragic or traumatic circumstances I experienced, the still small voice I could still hear within, and even the literature I read as an English major.

He has never been anything less than faithful to me; think of how faithful he is to you right now. Aren't you on the receiving end of his blessings on a daily basis? He remains faithful, even when you fail to acknowledge that every blessing you receive comes straight from his hand. You can trust him to be with you every minute of every day; he will never pull away from you on some capricious whim. Jeremiah expressed God's steadfastness this way: "Because of the LORD's great love we are not consumed, for his compassions never fail. They are new every morning; great is your faithfulness" (Lam. 3:22–23).

And of course, God's faithfulness to you extends into eternity. Like each believer in the Corinthian church to whom Paul wrote the letter that contains this verse—and those recipients were a group of sin-drenched Christians if there ever was one!—you will one day stand in the immediate presence of God as a blameless, righteous person because of your faith in Christ. You never need to fear the day when you will come face-to-face with the Lord. Not only will his faithfulness to you still be in effect, but it will also reach its perfect fulfillment on that day. You will see his trustworthiness more clearly than you ever could before.

In the meantime, you can show your faithfulness to God by remaining in that fellowship with Jesus Christ to which he called you. Responding to God's call is only the first step. He wants you to participate in a personal and intimate relationship with Christ, enjoying his presence and trusting him to guide you in the ways of God throughout the course of your life. His faithfulness to you is guaranteed; your faithfulness to him is the only appropriate response to such an awesome promise.

————

Lord, your compassions have never failed me, although I have failed to acknowledge them. Your faithfulness to me is immeasurable. Thank you for being a merciful and trustworthy God, yesterday, today, and tomorrow—and throughout eternity.

54

The Water and the Fire

When you pass through the waters,
I will be with you;
and when you pass through the rivers,
they will not sweep over you.
When you walk through the fire,
you will not be burned;
the flames will not set you ablaze.

Isaiah 43:2

HAVE you ever noticed how many times in the Bible God reminded his people of all that he had done for them? In the first section of Isaiah 43, the Lord expressed his love for the nation of Israel in part by recounting all the trials he had brought the Israelites through. And then he looked to the future, assuring them that what he had done for them in the past he would continue to do in the years to come.

What had he done for them? For starters, he brought the Israelites out of their captivity in Egypt and held back the waters of the Red Sea just long enough for them to pass through safely (Exod.

14:21–22). "When you pass through the waters," he promised in Isaiah, "I will be with you."

Likewise, when the Israelites completed their forty-year sojourn in the wilderness and were finally ready to enter the land that God promised them, the Lord dammed up the waters of the Jordan River so that the Israelites could cross the riverbed on dry ground (Josh. 3:15–17). Reminding them of that event through Isaiah, he promised, "When you pass through the rivers, they will not sweep over you."

Finally, God brought to mind the miracle he worked in the fiery furnace of King Nebuchadnezzar. When Israel walked through the fire the way Shadrach, Meshach, and Abednego did, he said, "you will not be burned; the flames will not set you ablaze" (see Dan. 3). These were hardly insignificant events in the history of the nation of Israel; God had always been there for them, to protect them from floods and fires and plagues and far more powerful armies.

What are some of the overwhelming deluges and fiery trials God has brought you through? Maybe he needs to remind you of those things so you can begin to believe that his protection in the past serves as an illustration of his promise to you for the future. Has he brought you through a broken relationship, a debilitating illness, a financial crisis? Hasn't he protected you time and again from losing hope, losing your life—losing it all? Look back on all that the Lord has done for you in years gone by and consider it a pledge for all that he will do for you in the years to come.

———

Lord, you have brought me through so much—the years I wasted serving the wrong master, attacks from my enemies, times of spiritual discouragement, illnesses, accidents, heartbreaks, much more than I can or even want to remember. But let me never forget your protection during those times. You've brought me safely through every ordeal.

55

God's Justice

He will judge the world in righteousness;
he will govern the peoples with justice.

Psalm 9:8

Iᶠ you ever want to get a clear picture of the way God administers justice, you need look no further than Genesis 18 and 19 and the story of the ancient city of Sodom. God had apparently been exceedingly patient with the people of Sodom, as the moral decline of the city had been taking place for some time. Finally, his patience ran out, and he threatened to destroy everyone in the city.

Abraham, though, had a personal stake in that declaration. His nephew Lot lived in Sodom with his family, so Abraham began to wonder whether God would kill the righteous people of the city along with the wicked. Through a series of questions, he established that if God could find a mere ten righteous people in Sodom, he would spare the city. But he could not. He allowed the few righteous people, including Lot, to escape, but he followed through with the annihilation of the rest of Sodom.

That punishment sounds harsh to us today. As people often ask, how can a loving God administer such a severe form of justice? What we fail to realize when we read stories like this one is that God in his sovereignty created the world for a purpose—and very early on, people began to abuse and disregard that purpose. The sin of Sodom, coming as early as it did in human history, was an affront to the righteousness of God. To allow Sodom to continue to exist in such a flagrant state of sinfulness—after repeated indications that he was about to unleash his wrath—would have undermined God's sovereignty.

In his second epistle, Peter explained that God destroyed Sodom, and its sister city in sin, Gomorrah, to set an example for the rest of humankind. Apparently it worked. While the intent was to show how seriously God judged blatant, willful sin, the story also underscored a principle that is equally important: that God does not want to consume the righteous along with the wicked. He provided a way of escape even then, two millennia before he sent his Son to reconcile the world to Himself, so that everyone could escape the punishment for sin.

People say they want to believe in a loving God, but in reality what they want is a weak and powerless God. God's administration of justice in no way negates his love. He will always give people every opportunity to turn from their wickedness and live according to the principles of right living that he has established. As one who has been reconciled to God through Christ, you have no need to fear his judgment. Your right living places you on the godly side of the scales of justice.

———

Lord, I may not always understand your ways, but I believe that your ways are always just and good. Thank you for sending Jesus Christ to reconcile the world to you.

56

Avenging Wrong

Do not take revenge, my friends, but leave room for God's wrath, for it is written: "It is mine to avenge; I will repay," says the Lord.

Romans 12:19

IF you are accustomed to an older translation of the Bible, you probably grew up hearing people quote this verse as "Vengeance is mine." But what God is promising here is to *avenge* wrong, not exact *vengeance*. There's a difference, and it's an important one—as is the admonition to us not to take *revenge*.

First, get rid of the idea that God is promising here to pay back those who have done you wrong. Vengeance implies lashing out at someone in a violent way, and although God is God and he can do that if he wants to, that's not the intended meaning of this verse.

Second, get rid of any notion that you should ever take matters into your own hands and take revenge against someone who has wronged you, regardless of how justified you feel you are. To take revenge is to turn your resentment toward someone into an opportunity to inflict pain or injury on that person. It's the antithesis of

Christian love, and besides that, it's completely out of your area of responsibility. And this is where the beauty of this promise comes in.

Rather than allow you to shoulder the responsibility of determining what kind of retribution your enemy deserves, God asks you to step aside so he can take it all on himself. And what God promises to do is *avenge* the wrong. Avenging a wrong does involve punishment, but it's one that stems from God's system of justice. It's not vindictive; it's simply right. When God avenges a wrong, you walk away with a sense of satisfaction that the right thing has been done to the wrongdoer. Neither vengeance nor revenge can provide that for you.

One of the best-known examples of God's promise to avenge the wrongs done to his people is found in the story of Ahab, a king of Israel, and his wife, Jezebel, in 1 Kings 16–21. An idol-worshiper, Jezebel systematically eliminated or drove out those priests of God who opposed her; Elijah, the prophet of God, countered by overseeing the slaying of all of her priests.

The clincher came when Jezebel's greed resulted in the death of an innocent man named Naboth, whose land she wanted and ultimately got. This time, God delivered a prophecy to a military commander named Jehu: "This is what the LORD, the God of Israel, says: 'I anoint you king over the LORD's people Israel. You are to destroy the house of Ahab your master, and I will avenge the blood of my servants the prophets and the blood of all the LORD's servants shed by Jezebel. The whole house of Ahab will perish. I will cut off from Ahab every last male in Israel—slave or free'" (2 Kings 9:6–8). A gruesome image follows, and the next thing you know, Ahab and Jezebel are indeed dead, and Jehu is indeed the king of Israel.

The freedom that Christ offers us takes so many distinct forms that we could probably never count them all. The freedom inherent in Romans 12:19 is this: We never have to worry about seeking retribution. We never have to be concerned about whether our means of avenging wrong is just. We never have to fear that we've gone too far—or not far enough—in punishing our enemies.

None of those responsibilities is ours to begin with. When we give our anger and resentment toward our enemies over to God, we can relax, knowing that the God of justice will work on our behalf to avenge the wrong that we have suffered.

————

Lord, thank you for freeing me from the responsibility of exacting vengeance on those who have hurt me. I am grateful that I can hand my enemies over to you, knowing that you will deal with them in a just and satisfying way. Keep me from ever being tempted to take matters of retribution into my own hands.

57

Invited Guest

Here I am! I stand at the door and knock. If anyone hears my voice and opens the door, I will come in and eat with him, and he with me.

Revelation 3:20

EVEN if you don't know the name Warner Sallman, you probably know his artwork. His *Head of Christ* is among the best-known images of Jesus, and his *Christ at Heart's Door* is often used to depict the promise in Revelation 3:20. These two prints adorned the walls in the Methodist church of my childhood, and I never doubted that they were faithful representations of the Lord. I've since modified my notion of what Jesus might have looked like, just as I've reexamined the meaning of Revelation 3:20.

You may have grown up believing, as I did, that this verse indicates that Christ is waiting to be invited in to a person's life. In other words, it's a verse related to salvation. But look at it again, with fresh eyes; some scholars now believe that it's actually a verse about fellowship.

Consider this interpretation: Jesus is standing at the door as a guest, awaiting your offer of hospitality. He hears what's going on inside, and he wants to be a part of that, but he's not one to barge right in and crash the party. All he wants is to spend time with you, sharing a meal and delighting in your presence—but he wants you to want him there.

That's a heady thought; there's the Lord himself, promising to hang out with you if you'll only ask him. You shouldn't be so surprised, though, when you look at how much of his time on Earth he spent with his friends and companions. He seems to have been a frequent guest at all kinds of banquets and feasts and dinners. He clearly enjoyed sharing a meal with others; in fact, he comes across as downright relaxed when he was "reclining at the table," as some Bible versions describe his laid-back demeanor.

Imagine a totally relaxed Jesus, reclining—okay, in our culture he'd be sitting—at your table, eating, drinking, laughing, asking you to pass the mashed potatoes. It shouldn't be all that hard, because when *you* are sitting at your table—eating, drinking, laughing, passing the mashed potatoes—he's right there with you, if you have already made him a part of your life. Invite him to make his presence known to you, and enjoy the fellowship and communion he offers.

Make Jesus the Lord of your everyday life. Allow him to share the fun times with you as well as the devotional times. Don't leave him waiting outside, knocking on the door. The Lord of all creation wants to unwind with you—you! Extend the invitation. You can count on him to come in.

———

Lord, never let me keep you waiting outside my door. Do whatever it takes to get my attention, because I cannot think of a higher honor than to have you cross the threshold of my life.

58

Bond of Love

For I am convinced that neither death nor life, neither angels nor demons, neither the present nor the future, nor any powers, neither height nor depth, nor anything else in all creation, will be able to separate us from the love of God that is in Christ Jesus our Lord.

Romans 8:38–39

I F you are already familiar with this passage, chances are you occasionally overlook the five-word phrase that ends Paul's string of "neither . . . nor" constructions. But it's in that five-word phrase— "anything else in all creation"—that the most powerful message lies.

Consider that phrase to be the ultimate fill-in-the-blank promise. Go ahead: try to come up with a word that does *not* fit the description of "anything else." You cannot do it, just as you cannot be separated from the love of God that is in Christ Jesus your Lord.

I confess that I didn't always pay attention to those five words. The rest of the neither/nors were so spiritual or so abstract ("neither height nor depth"?) that I would read the remainder of the passage as if it trailed right off the page. But I was brought up short one day when I reread the verse and substituted the word *depression* for "anything else." Not even depression could separate a believer from the love of God? That's right. And that's when this powerful promise became real to me.

What is it in your life that at times causes you to doubt God's love? It's all well and good to acknowledge the impotence of angels and demons compared to the love of God, but it may be much harder to render the same degree of powerlessness to those things that threaten to undo you. If there's a sin, a habit, an attitude, an area of doubt that you feel has walled off God's love from you, you can be assured that God is not the one who put up the barrier. Those things may hinder your communion with God and your enjoyment of him, but no sin, no habit, no attitude, no area of doubt has the power to stand between you and the love God has for you.

God knows how hard we can be on ourselves, and he knows how much we need to be reassured that he will not withdraw his love from us just because we've messed up or, even worse, just because he feels like it. Whenever you find yourself questioning God's love, remember this verse and the promise it contains. And don't allow that all-important five-word phrase to trail off the page as you read it. Those words hold a powerful promise, one that can help you bask in his overwhelming love once again.

———

Lord, remind me to fill in those blanks when I begin to think I've done something that would remove your love from me. Keep me mindful of the fact that nothing can separate me from your love.

59

A Lasting Covenant

I will not violate my covenant
or alter what my lips have uttered.

Psalm 89:34

GOD'S promises would not amount to much if he weren't trustworthy. He could promise you the moon and the stars, the universe itself, but it would not mean a thing if you did not have the assurance that he would keep his word. Thank God—literally—that that's not the case.

The Bible, of course, is saturated with verses that attest to the trustworthiness of God. Several verses in Psalms confirm the trustworthiness of his Word. "The law of the LORD is perfect, reviving the soul. The statutes of the LORD are trustworthy making wise the simple," David wrote in Psalm 19:7. Another psalmist—or other psalmists—agreed; the writer of Psalm 117 expressed it like this: "The works of his hands are faithful and just; all his precepts are trustworthy" (verse 7), while the author of Psalm 119 made sure to include two verses underscoring the same idea: "All your commands are trustworthy" (verse 86) and "The statutes you have laid down are righteous; they are fully trustworthy" (verse 138). His very character guarantees that he will follow through on his promises. And then there are verses like Psalm 89:34, in which God comes right out and states that he will not renege on what he has promised.

What he has promised, of course, is spelled out in the covenants, or agreements, God has made with individuals, with the nation of Israel, and with the followers of Christ. While this verse applies specifically to the covenant God made with David, the underlying truth—that God will not "alter what [his] lips have uttered"—also applies generally to all of God's covenants.

To King David, he promised a continuation of his royal lineage—culminating in the birth of the person of Jesus Christ, the Messiah. And it was through Christ that God sealed his covenant with the Lord's followers. That covenant holds out the promise of salvation by grace, God's unmerited favor. God's words in Psalm 89:34 assure us that he will never violate or rescind that agreement. We need not live in fear that he will one day rethink his offer of grace and suddenly require us to jump through a succession of religious hoops to earn our salvation. We can serve him in confidence, knowing that he is not some fickle deity bent on tripping us up at every turn.

Likewise, we have the assurance that God will not up and change those things that he has said to his people down through the centuries. What God has spoken will come to pass. We can know with certainty that he will fulfill every promise in the Bible because God will not change the words he has already given us.

What does all this mean in our daily lives? It means that we can wait in patient expectation. Our every hope depends on the trustworthiness of God and the covenant he has made with us. We can stand on his word, knowing that God stands behind his Word.

———

Lord, I thank you that you are a God I can trust. Help me to remember that as I wait to see your promises fulfilled. And give me the grace and power to be trustworthy in making good on the words I speak and the promises I make to you and to others.

60

Wordless Prayer

In the same way, the Spirit helps us in our weakness. We do not know what we ought to pray for, but the Spirit himself intercedes for us with groans that words cannot express.

Romans 8:26

HAVE you ever experienced a situation so troubling that you couldn't find the words to express your feelings? Maybe a friend wronged you, a loved one rejected you, or a doctor diagnosed you with a debilitating disease. And when bad things like that happen to the good people in your life, you can find yourself equally speechless. You try to pray, but the words just won't come. All too often, you feel as if you are somehow inadequate; certainly as a believer you should be able to pray—right?

Instead of berating yourself for your inability to pray, take heart in the promise found in Romans 8:26. God knew well ahead of time that you would face difficult or bewildering situations that would render you incapable of translating the cry of your heart into mere words. He sent the Holy Spirit to accomplish what language cannot; the Spirit himself prays "with groans that words cannot express," which makes it pretty clear that what is inadequate is human language—not you. As expressive as language can be, words do occasionally come up against their limitations. So the Holy Spirit—who is not confined to time, space, and language—begins to take over where you are forced to leave off.

Not only is the Holy Spirit praying for you, he is also connecting you to God by interceding for you. Your inability to pray may make you feel as if you are cut off from the Father, outside the range of his hearing. That's when the Spirit's work of prayerful intercession provides the much-needed assurance that your unspoken pleas will not go unheard. Your heart-cry is loud enough for him to hear and interpret.

Realize, too, that it's not important that you understand how he does this. All you need to do is pour your heart out to God in whatever way you can. The Holy Spirit is ready, willing, and able to say what you can't. Let him do the work God sent him to do.

God is a compassionate and understanding Father who is well aware of our weaknesses. He knows that life can become so overwhelming that we simply do not know how to pray. And he has not left us to sort things out on our own. He sent the Holy Spirit to fill in when we find ourselves without a prayer. That's a promise you can draw on without saying a word.

―――――

Thank you, Lord, for sending the Holy Spirit to intercede on my behalf and give expression to the prayers that I cannot utter. Remind me to relax and allow the Spirit to transform my unspoken words into groans that you fully understand.

61

A Forgetting God

I, even I, am he who blots out your transgressions,
for my own sake,
and remembers your sin no more.

Isaiah 43:25

WHAT image comes to mind when you contemplate God's power to forgive your sins? Do you see him as a celestial judge, pounding a gavel and proclaiming you "Not guilty!"—in a deep, authoritative voice, of course? That image, however preposterous it may sound, is not far from the way some believers have mistakenly come to think of God.

The forty-third chapter of Isaiah presents an image of God that far surpasses that of a mere judge. As God so clearly points out, he is ultimately the one we sin against—hardly the case with an earthly judge. And we do it so frequently, so consistently, that a lesser god would have given up on us long ago. But he does not abandon us to our folly, even though, as he stated in the second part of verse 24, "You have burdened me with your sins and wearied me with your offenses."

In the very next verse he made this astonishing promise: he will blot out our transgressions and remember our sin no more. *Why would he do that?* Why would he be so merciful, forgiving, and kind to those people who turn their backs on him? He does it to keep his covenant with his people, the people he loves, the people who continue to sin against him.

This verse expresses what Bible teacher John MacArthur considers to be the "high point of grace"[1] in the Old Testament, and there probably aren't too many people who would disagree with him. What an incredible promise! God does not just forgive our sins, he cancels them altogether. His willingness to make an intentional point of forgetting our transgressions is nothing short of, well, divine.

What this verse means, of course, is that we never have to worry that one day God will dredge up some heinous transgression from our past and parade it around the neighborhood for everyone to see. We will never hear him bring up our "priors," as an earthly judge would: "Well, I see you have quite a record, dating back to . . . hmmm, the day you were born. The court has no choice but to sentence you to hard labor this time!" No, God will not bring up your previous record, because to him, you don't have one. The blood of Jesus Christ has covered your sins, permanently blotting them out. And God remembers them no more.

———

Lord, your grace and mercy are greater than I can possibly comprehend; never let me take your kindness for granted. Thank you, thank you, for erasing and forgetting the record of my sins. Now grant me the grace to treat others the way you treat me, never dredging up their past wrongs against me but consciously forgetting what I claim to have forgiven.

62

Emissaries from God

For he will command his angels concerning you
to guard you in all your ways;
they will lift you up in their hands,
so that you will not strike your foot against a stone.

Psalm 91:11–12

CONTRARY to the predictions of many naysayers, interest in an-gels—which experienced a renewal just prior to the turn of the millennium—remains at a high level. That's good, to some extent; it's an indication that people have become more inclined to develop a spiritual perspective on things. But to a great extent, that's not so good, because many people lack a genuine understanding of angels and their ministry. It's hard to think of the "angel on my shoulder" as little more than a sweet, comforting presence, which is a far cry from what the Scriptures portray.

The angels depicted in the Bible are mighty, powerful beings who operate at the command and discretion of God. Their ministry to believers includes delivering messages from God (Acts 8:26, 10:3–7), offering comfort and guidance (Acts 27:22–25; Matt. 18:10; Heb. 1:14)—and providing protection, according to Psalm 91:11–12.

That's a powerful promise, one that Satan failed to take seriously. He twisted it and tried to use it to tempt Jesus in Matthew 4, to no avail, of course.

Because angels seldom announce their presence, it's usually difficult to appreciate their ministry. But once you accept by faith the "evidence of things not seen" (Heb. 11:1 NKJV)—in this case, angelic beings—you may find that you are becoming acutely aware of the many times they have protected you from danger, injury, or worse. If you've ever arrived home from work to discover that a multiple-car pileup occurred minutes after you drove on that stretch of road, you have good reason to believe that an angel or two was looking out for you.

Angels also offer spiritual protection (Ps. 34:7), delivering you from tempting situations far more often than you can imagine. Maybe you struggle with the sin of lust; just in the nick of time, a mighty angelic being comes to your rescue, standing between you and that object of your misguided affection—whether it be a woman, man, or a bakery case full of tempting sweets. Perhaps your downfall is pride; unknown to you, an angel keeps you from discovering a juicy little tidbit about your competitor, forcing you to deal with the juicy little tidbits in your own life.

Keep in mind, though, that it's God who deserves your thanks and praise for the work the angels perform on your behalf. He's the one who created them, gives them their power, and sends them to minister to you. They are well aware of that and will always direct your eyes away from themselves and onto him, where they rightfully belong.

———

Lord, thank you for sending your ministering angels to take care of me. Give me the faith to believe that they are always on the job, even though I may not always recognize their activity.

63

The Way They Should Go

Train a child in the way he should go,
and when he is old he will not turn from it.

Proverbs 22:6

THIS is one promise that baffles many a parent. Maybe you're one of them. You want to believe that your child will follow the Lord, but you see little evidence of a desire for the things of God in his life. You feel as if you've done all the right things that should have produced all the right results. Yet your eight-year-old uses language that you never used, even in your wildest days; your teenager dresses in a way that you never dressed, even in your wildest days; and your adult offspring—well, that's another story, and not one you want to tell.

Training children to follow God involves much more than taking them to church and Sunday school, sending them to a Christian school, or encouraging them to take part in a youth group and other age-appropriate activities in the church. It involves investing time and energy in the shaping of their character through direct means, such as instructing and guiding them, and indirect means, such as modeling godly behavior and praying for wisdom as a parent, guardian, or other adult role model.

Notice, too, that the promise in Proverbs 22:6 applies to children who have been trained "in the way [they] should go." In a general sense, that "way" is fairly straightforward: teach your children to trust God and obey him, seeking his will for their lives and desiring to please him in all they do. But in another, more specific sense, each child needs to be trained in the *personal* way he or she should go.

That kind of personal training requires sacrifice and effort on your part. It involves going before God, who knows your child inside and out in a way you never will, and asking him for a greater insight into your child's nature. It means tailoring the training to each child's particular needs instead of using a universal, cookie-cutter approach. Sound daunting? Good parenting always is, but relying on God for wisdom and guidance at the outset makes it infinitely more rewarding.

If you're still not convinced that this promise could ever apply to you, look at the second part of the verse. Chances are, your children are not "old" yet. They may still be in training, even if they are teenagers or young adults. You may see a wayward son; God sees a young man with a heart crying out to him, a heart that will eventually turn toward him.

Hold on to this promise, no matter what is going on in your children's lives. Never, ever give up on your children. God never gave up on you, and he holds out the same hope for your offspring.

———

Lord, show me how to train the children you have entrusted to me, and give me the faith to believe that they will not depart from your ways. Thank you for never giving up on them—or on me.

64

An Astonishing Act

How great is the love the Father has lavished on us, that we should be called children of God! And that is what we are! The reason the world does not know us is that it did not know him.

1 John 3:1

IN one of his recent hit songs, Christian singer and songwriter Steven Curtis Chapman declared that he was "amazed," "astonished," and downright "speechless" at the love of God.[1] Specifically, the lyrics in Chapman's "Speechless" refer directly to the love of God as the apostle John expressed it in this verse. It's an appropriate image, because the original language expresses nothing less than awe at the depth of a divine love that would grant family status to the merely mortal.

This kind of love is indeed "lavished"—how better to describe the action involved? God has granted you the unparalleled privilege of being born again into the family of God.

Inherent in your status as a natural-born child of God is a host of promises, starting with the assurance that your family relationship is a permanent one. Your Father will always be your Father. Because he is a loving Father by nature, he will always delight in you as his child. And if your earthly father failed to be the kind of parent you wanted and needed, you now have a perfect Father who will never abuse, disappoint, or abandon you.

So here you are, a child of God and a member of his "forever family." How is it that no one outside this family seems to recognize your special relationship to the Creator of the universe? The rest of the verse addresses that question. The "world"—those who are outside of the family—does not recognize the existence, presence, or authority of God; it cannot possibly recognize the status of those humans whom God has claimed as his own. That includes you. You can't expect people to identify your kinship with God when they can't comprehend the possibility of a relationship with him.

God will fulfill the promises he made to you as his child largely outside the view of the world. You may go through your life perfectly tuned in to the many blessings God has bestowed on you, but those beyond the family may dismiss those blessings as coincidence or chance. You will know better, because you recognize the existence, presence, and authority—but especially, the astonishing depth of the love—of God.

———

Father! I am so grateful that I can legitimately call you Father! Thank you for making me your natural-born child, bringing me in to a permanent family relationship with you. I stand before you, astonished and amazed and speechless at this love that you have lavished upon me.

65

A Sentry over Your Heart and Mind

Do not be anxious about anything, but in everything, by prayer and petition, with thanksgiving, present your requests to God. And the peace of God, which transcends all understanding, will guard your hearts and minds in Christ Jesus.

Philippians 4:6–7

WHATEVER defined our cultural tendency toward anxiety changed on September 11, 2001. Those things that traditionally contributed to our anxious thoughts—crime, the economy, and disease, among others—paled in comparison to the reality, and the very real future threat, of terrorism.

Bioterrorism, weapons of mass destruction, smart bombs, and *chemical warfare* have since become everyday terms in front-page news stories. Osama bin Laden and al-Qaeda are part of our lexicon. Airline travel, once considered secure and immune to danger, has become a nightmare for many who live with the fear that some crazed extremist will find yet another way to sabotage the system. And a year after anthrax spores contaminated the postal service, authorities were no closer to naming a suspect than they were in the days following the deaths of a half-dozen anthrax victims.

What all this means is that we as a nation have acquired an additional layer of anxiety, piled on top of countless layers of individual and personal concerns that each of us deals with on a daily basis. How can God's promise of peace in Philippians 4:7 possibly penetrate all of that and find its way into our hearts and minds? What hope do we have that our lives will ever be free of the countless reasons—both real and imagined—that compel us to live in a constant state of worry?

The answers to those questions start with our responsibility in verse 6. Paul told us that we should not be anxious about anything, but we should keep bringing our concerns to God in prayer, with an attitude of thankfulness. We need to be sensitive to those things that create anxiety in our lives, eliminate as many as we can, and place the rest in the hands of God.

When we do that, the promise kicks in. That's when God, in essence, sets a sentry over our hearts and minds, filling us with a peace that "transcends all understanding." "Transcends" means that his peace exists not only above our understanding but also apart from it. We simply cannot fathom that kind of peace even as we access and experience it. But God doesn't ask us to comprehend it. He just wants us to enjoy it.

When your anxious thoughts threaten to overwhelm you, pray about your concerns. Give yourself the opportunity to draw on that indescribable peace, and allow God to set that guard over your heart and mind. And remember to thank him for it.

MARCIA FORD

———

Lord, I want to experience the peace that transcends all understanding. I give you everything that causes me anxiety. Thank you for your promise of a peace that is so awesome that I cannot even grasp it.

66

The Power of Persistent Prayer

So I say to you: Ask and it will be given to you; seek and you will find; knock and the door will be opened to you. For everyone who asks receives; he who seeks finds; and to him who knocks, the door will be opened.

Luke 11:9–10

HAVE you ever had this uneasy feeling that you're nagging God, actually pestering him in prayer? Don't worry about it. God can handle your tenacity. In fact, he welcomes it, and this verse provides proof.

Right before Jesus made this promise, he gave his disciples a lesson in prayer and followed that with a story about the power of persistent prayer. The lesson is embedded in Jesus' expression of the model prayer in Luke 11:2–4, the one we have come to call the Lord's Prayer. The story begins in the next verse: "Then he said to them, 'Suppose one of you has a friend, and he goes to him at midnight and says, "Friend, lend me three loaves of bread, because a friend of mine on a journey has come to me, and I have nothing to set before him." Then the one inside answers, "Don't bother me. The door is already locked, and my children are with me in bed. I can't get up and give you anything." I tell you, though he will not get up and give him the bread because he is his friend, yet because of the man's boldness he will get up and give him as much as he needs'" (Luke 11:5–8).

Verse 9 comes immediately after, and its three verbs imply continuous action. In fact, the *Amplified Bible* translates the verbs as "ask *and* keep on asking . . . seek *and* keep on seeking . . . knock *and* keep on knocking." It's apparent that you can "keep on" asking, seeking, and knocking with the assurance that you will receive what you ask for, find what you seek, and have the right door open up for you.

Bear in mind that when Jesus decided to make this promise in the same context as the Lord's Prayer, it's likely that he expected his disciples to have the spirit of that prayer fresh in their minds. That means we should always utter our prayers in submission to the will of God ("Your will be done," Matt. 6:10). You can ask for a million dollars, seek to know the future, and knock on the door of forbidden opportunity, but those prayers are not likely to be in accordance with God's will. The promise applies to those who persist in prayer for those things that please God.

Your continual pleading is no irritation to the Father, who loves you and loves to hear you communicating with him. Unlike a grumpy, sleep-deprived friend, he is up all night anyway, and his larder is always full. He promises to answer your requests. Keep on asking, keep on seeking, keep on knocking, even if you feel as if you're nagging him. He can take it, and he wants to give you all that he has for you.

———

Father, thank you for promising to answer my relentless prayers. Remind me always to pray in the spirit of the prayer your Son modeled for us when he was on Earth—to pray according to your will on Earth as well as your will for my life.

67

We Shall Be Like Him

Dear friends, now we are children of God, and what we will be has not yet been made known. But we know that when he appears, we shall be like him, for we shall see him as he is.

1 John 3:2

ABOUT the highest compliment you could ever receive is that you are a person of Christlike character. When someone makes that kind of observation, she is saying that you have behaved or handled a situation in much the same way that Jesus would—with wisdom, compassion, and kindness, among other qualities. Maybe you don't feel that you would ever qualify for that kind of compliment. No matter. The Bible promises that one day in the future, you *will* be like Jesus, because on this day in the present, you are a child of God.

That day in the future will come when he reappears, and the whole world will see him for who he really is. Though there's plenty of disagreement over how the events of his return will line up, there's no disputing that every believer will be transformed in some way. "What we will be has not yet been made known," the apostle John wrote, and he left it at that. It's enough to know that each child of God will reflect the glory of God and the character of Christ; further speculation is unnecessary.

In the meantime, there's no reason why you can't practice developing those Christlike qualities here on Earth. The people in your everyday life may just be looking for evidence of God's influence on you, and your new and improved character is one of the best ways to show them that God is already changing you into the image of Jesus.

What does it mean to be Christlike on Earth? In part, it means behaving in a way that will bring honor and glory to God. It means exhibiting the attributes of a true follower of Christ, listed in part in 2 Peter 1:5–7: faith, virtue, knowledge, self-control, perseverance, godliness, brotherly kindness, and love. There are other attributes, of course; all you need to do is look at the person of Jesus Christ to acquire a clear picture of the ideal way in which his followers should conduct their lives.

Will you fall short of that ideal? Of course you will; everyone does. But you can hold on to the promise that one day, when Jesus returns, you will be so changed that your very nature will be like his. And you won't even care if no one pays you that ultimate compliment.

———

Lord, I look forward to the day when you return and I will be like you. Until then, I ask that you give me the grace to allow you to reshape my character so that it more closely resembles yours.

68

A New Baptism

I baptize you with water for repentance. But after me will come one who is more powerful than I, whose sandals I am not fit to carry. He will baptize you with the Holy Spirit and with fire.

Matthew 3:11

JOHN the Baptist spoke these words after he noticed that many of the religious leaders of his day—the Pharisees and Sadducees—had come to witness his ritual of baptizing his followers in the Jordan River. After clarifying that he was doing so only for those who repented of their sins, he issued both a promise and a warning: the worthy one who would come after him would baptize his followers with the Holy Spirit—and those who rejected him, with fire (v. 12). He very pointedly directed his remarks at the pompous leaders who would ultimately refuse to accept Jesus as the Messiah.

The people who stood on the banks of the Jordan that day could not appreciate that promise as you can today. Not until the Holy Spirit descended at Pentecost, as Acts 2 describes, could believers fully understand what the ministry of the Holy Spirit would mean in their lives. Even today, many Christians fail to recognize the fulfillment of this promise on a personal level.

When Jesus has baptized you in the Holy Spirit, the Spirit indwells you and begins his work of regeneration and sanctification in your life (see Titus 3:5; 1 Cor. 6:11). Your rebirth is both a one-time event and an ongoing process, as you daily draw on the power of the Holy Spirit for spiritual renewal. Through his work of sanctification, the Spirit sets you apart as a consecrated person with the power to lead a life of holiness.

As if that weren't enough, the Spirit also equips you for service to God by imparting spiritual gifts (1 Cor. 12), providing revelation into the meaning of God's Word and into his specific will for your life (1 Cor. 2:10–13), and interceding in prayer on your behalf (Rom. 8:26).

There's more, of course, much more. John 14–16 tells us that the ministry of the Holy Spirit includes comfort, bearing witness to the divine Sonship of Christ, and guiding you into "all truth" (John 16:13). And it is the Spirit, the third person of the Trinity, who convicts the world of sin (John 16:9) and leads people to repentance.

Walk out the reality of this promise in your day-to-day life by submitting yourself to the ministry of the Holy Spirit, allowing him to continue the good work that he began in you on the day you first believed. Use the power of the Spirit to live a sanctified life of service to God the Father. And be thankful that God gave you the wisdom to embrace Jesus as the Messiah—wisdom that far surpasses that of the Pharisees and Sadducees.

———

Lord, thank you for sending the Holy Spirit to indwell and empower me. Open my eyes so that I may recognize his ongoing work in my life and the many ways he ministers to me each day.

69

Security in an Insecure World

My people will live in peaceful dwelling places,
in secure homes,
in undisturbed places of rest.

Isaiah 32:18

WITHIN a year after the September 11 attacks on the World Trade Center and the Pentagon, the Bush administration established a new arm of the government, the Department of Homeland Security. Along with the FBI and the CIA—whose best intelligence failed them at a most critical time—this new department was designed in part to give Americans a much-needed sense of safety in the wake of the unprecedented horror they had just experienced.

To be sure, the government had to do something to forestall the potential panic that the threat of violence could provoke, and creating a new agency to fight terrorism was probably as good a move as any they could have made at that time. But even if the United States were to gather every monetary and military resource at its disposal and commit it to fighting the war on terrorism, the government would never be able to give its citizens what they truly need to live in peaceful dwelling places: an unshakable source of security that has withstood the test of time.

The needs of the people of the United States, of course, are no different from those of everyone else who has ever lived. People everywhere and at all times have needed a reason to believe their homes were protected, that their places of rest would be undisturbed. But no government established by humankind has ever been able to make that guarantee. And no government ever will.

God, however, makes that promise. But how can he? How can he assure you that you will be able to live in peace and security in the midst of such a turbulent world? He can make that promise because the security he offers is the kind that comes only from within. When the Spirit of God indwells you, his protection is accessible to you; all you need to do is call on him. He also can make that promise because he himself is an unshakable source of security that has withstood the test of time—and will continue to do so throughout eternity.

All around you are people who live in fear and uncertainty—many more so since terrorism shattered the illusion that they were safe. You can be a witness to them of the peace that comes from knowing God and counting on him to keep you calm and assured when the world around you borders on chaos. No security force on Earth can make that guarantee.

————

Lord, thank you for being my shelter, all that I will ever need. Keep me from looking to others, including the government, for the kind of peace and protection that only you can provide. I am trusting you alone to allow me to dwell in a place of peacefulness, security, and undisturbed rest.

70

Never Give Up

Being confident of this, that he who began a good work in you will carry it on to completion until the day of Christ Jesus.

Philippians 1:6

HAVE you ever felt like quitting, just packing it all in? Your life as a believer may have become too hard with too few visible results. You aren't in such bad shape that you would walk away from the Lord entirely, but you are in a condition that makes you feel useless, drained, and too tired to go on. You are tempted to give up your responsibilities in the church or in other areas of service to God, to give up on daily devotions, to give up on trying to live your version of the Christian life.

Nearly all Christians face that type of discouragement from time to time. You look at your life and think you should be farther along on the path of faith than you are. You judge your "success" as a Christian by all kinds of external factors, such as the number of people you have led to the Lord or the amount of time you can spend in prayer before your mind starts to wander.

Yet you are quick to counsel others against judging by appearances. "Man looks at the outward appearance, but the LORD looks at the heart," you say, quoting 1 Samuel 16:7. Meanwhile, you are doing to yourself exactly what you tell people not to do to others. All along, God is looking at your heart, your hunger and thirst for him, your desire to please him, even your misguided efforts to apply standards to your spiritual life that God never sanctioned. He sees that your heart is turned toward him, that you do so much with the intention of furthering the cause of Christ on Earth. He is pleased with what he sees, even if you are not.

More importantly, he is maturing you in ways you cannot recognize. But if you have been with the Lord for any significant amount of time, you can no doubt look back on where you were when you first began your walk with him and where you are now. You think you should be miles farther down the road, but you may be much farther along than you realize.

Let God be the judge of your level of maturity. And trust him to fulfill his promise to complete the good work he started in you. Yield to him and allow him to continue to transform you in the way and in the time frame he sees fit. Above all, don't give up on yourself; he certainly hasn't, and he never will.

———

Lord, thank you for bringing me as far along on this journey of faith as you have. I believe that you are doing a good work in me and through me, and that you will not abandon that work.

71

Humbling Yourself

Humble yourselves before the Lord, and he will lift you up.

James 4:10

THIS promise is one that is almost guaranteed to make you think: first of all, about what it means to humble yourself, and second, about whether you should expect the Lord to "lift you up" or exalt you. Do you have to think of yourself as a lowly worm in order to be considered humble? And isn't it wrong to want to be exalted?

In the first place, humbling yourself doesn't mean you walk around in sackcloth and ashes, muttering "I am nobody" to everyone you meet. It means that when you see yourself in light of who God is, the sight humbles you. You can strut around acting like somebody special all you like, but the moment you stand in the presence of the holy Creator of the universe, well, you begin to see the word *special* in a whole new way. "Humble yourselves" implies an action on your part, though. You intentionally place yourself in a position relative to God—and that means you place yourself in submission to him.

When you do that, you lose any human desire to be exalted. You know that there is only one who is worthy of exaltation, and it is not you. As you stand in the presence of God, thoughts of yourself, your needs, and your concerns begin to evaporate completely. Your focus becomes riveted on him; your puny concerns begin to disappear as your self-centeredness gives way to God-centeredness.

Acknowledging your humble submission to him, God exalts you, or lifts you up, to a place of prominence. Perhaps he gives you an added measure of spiritual responsibility, a new ministry, or favor in the eyes of your boss. You may be completely astonished; you start to wonder, *What on Earth did I do to deserve this?* Well, nothing, but you did plenty in the spiritual realm. Then, of course, you are further humbled, and the next thing you know you are further blessed. God likes it when his people keep that kind of cycle going.

It's only those who humble themselves in submission to God whom he will exalt. To be counted among those, learn to look at yourself standing before a holy God. Humility should follow quickly enough.

———

Lord, I don't seek to be exalted. I seek only to see you high and lifted up, exalted above everything in heaven and on Earth. Teach me to see myself only in relation to you, submitted to you and obedient to your Word. I want nothing for myself but to remain in your presence forever.

72

Have Fun—and Be Holy

If a man cleanses himself from [ignoble purposes], he will be an instrument for noble purposes, made holy, useful to the Master and prepared to do any good work.

2 Timothy 2:21

It's probably a fair assumption that you've never thought of yourself as "an instrument for noble purposes, made holy, useful to the Master and prepared to do any good work." That's not surprising, either, because holiness—which is what this verse is ultimately about—is not exactly a hot sermon topic in our society. In fact, if you can remember the last time you heard holiness discussed in any context at all, you must have an excellent memory.

The reality is that "holiness" sounds, well, old-fashioned. The word evokes images of grim and somber-looking party poopers whose main goal in life is to shame others into joining their separated little clan. This would not be an image that resonates with America in the new millennium.

Our faulty definition of the word, though, does not invalidate the concept. God is holy, and he wants his people to be holy, too. Is that too much to ask? Well . . . yes, if holiness is a goal you have to attain on your own.

As usual, God does not expect us to accomplish the impossible. God is the one who sanctifies us and separates us from the power that sin once had over our lives. He performs the work of purification, consecrating us to a life of holiness and godliness. And he empowers us to resist temptation and avoid those things that threaten to introduce impurity into our newly cleansed lives.

God promises that once you have cleansed yourself and renounced ungodliness, he will fashion you into an instrument, or vessel, for his noble purposes. If you have a genuine love for God, that's what you want to be: a person who is useful to the Master and always ready to serve him. No need for a last-minute scrub with a disinfectant; you are pure and prepared.

It's time we all got rid of our stodgy and inaccurate image of what holiness is. To be holy is to allow others to see Christ in us. He was never the New Testament party pooper; that role fell to the Pharisees, who were among the first to give holiness a bad name. Like no one else, Jesus showed us how we can live a full life, surrounded by friends, family—even sinners!—and festivities of all kinds, and still maintain our purity. It's not impossible. God has given us everything we need to make it happen.

———

Lord, I know you want me to live a life that is holy and pleasing to you—and I know that's the best possible way to live. Keep me from returning to the negative view of holiness I've acquired over the years. Transform me into a "noble instrument" that is constantly available and useful to you. I want to remain ready to serve you.

73

Your Part in an Eternal Drama

There is surely a future hope for you,
and your hope will not be cut off.

Proverbs 23:18

WHAT is your hope for the future? Not the things you wish for—such as lots of money, world peace, good health—but the dream that finds its home in the yearnings of your heart. Can you even articulate what that is? Many of us can't; we become tongue-tied as we grope for a way to explain those things that lie deep inside of us. Words prove to be an inadequate means of getting the depth of the message across.

Author John Eldredge describes our hope as the profound awareness that we were created for something more than *this*, whatever our daily life looks like. God created us to be part of a larger drama set on a larger stage—the story of redemption that God has been telling ever since the moment he created the first man and woman.

We get glimpses of this future hope throughout our lives, sometimes in fleeting moments of pure bliss that we wish could last forever. In those moments, we absolutely know we are a part of that larger story, and that our role—no matter how small it may seem—is meaningful, significant, and vital to moving the plot along. We may just be an understudy, but when it's time to join the unfolding drama taking place on the stage of history, then every moment we spent waiting in the wings proves its value and worth.

How can we ever see our puny lives in terms of the larger unfolding of redemptive history? Whether we can see it or not—and I suspect God keeps us from seeing it for a very good reason—the seemingly mundane decisions we make often have greater consequences than we will ever know. A simple change of jobs could set into motion a series of life-changing actions in the lives of others, such as the person who took the job you vacated or the house you vacated when you accepted a transfer to another city. Each person affected by your decision will be coming in to a new environment, with new prospects and new relationships—and quite possibly, a new opportunity to come to faith. What's more, even though you've moved on, you've left behind a witness for Christ that could change the life of someone who once brushed you off. You can't see the larger unfolding drama, only your "little" part in it.

Proverbs 23:18 promises that you have this future hope, this hope that you will find a place in the unwritten story of redemption, just as so many believers found a place in the written story of redemption—the Bible. And in the meantime, God has not left you without hope for the here and now. Your "future hope" is not just for heaven and eternal life. It's also for your literal tomorrow, that your day-to-day life on earth can be both full and meaningful as you find God at work in the midst of it.

Look at Proverbs 23:18 again; this verse also promises that your hope will not be "cut off." You need never be afraid that God will change the terms of the promise or rescind it altogether. You can count on him to keep this promise valid for as long as he does all his promises: forever.

———

Lord, I feel this hope in the pit of my being that you created me for more than I am experiencing right now. I ask that you become so active and alive in my life that I will sense my role in the unfolding story of redemption that you continue to convey to me. Thank you for using me to move the story along, even though my part seems small. I trust that with you, even the insignificant can produce great and mighty results.

74

A Divine Inheritance

Praise be to the God and Father of our Lord Jesus Christ! In his great mercy he has given us new birth into a living hope through the resurrection of Jesus Christ from the dead, and into an inheritance that can never perish, spoil or fade.

1 Peter 1:3–4

It isn't enough that God provides us with eternal life and an eternal dwelling place, he also keeps in heaven an imperishable inheritance for us that will never spoil or fade. No matter how long our lives are on earth, our personal inheritance remains intact and awaits our arrival. There's no way it will diminish in value over time, or that God will hand it over to someone whose demise precedes ours. He keeps our inheritance in reserve for us.

That inheritance comprises all that belongs to God, because God, of course, possesses everything. But the awesome part of this promise is not so much the legacy itself as the fact that we are heirs at all. Us! The ungrateful, unappreciative created beings who became beneficiaries only because the Father sacrificed his beloved Son and grants the inheritance to those who believe in his Son's completed work on the cross. What kind of deal is that for the Father?

It's nearly impossible to equate our inheritance in heaven with the earthly kind some of us may receive from our parents or other relatives and loved ones. No matter how large a person's estate is, the dollar value is a finite amount, so no matter how big a share of the estate we receive, our portion will also be a finite amount.

And what about those with whom we must share our earthly inheritance? Every name in our benefactor's will reduces the size of our take, which is one of the infrequently mentioned causes for so much tension in blended families. *What right do they have to muscle in on our rights as the original heirs? What kind of deal is that for us?*

Thankfully, we'll never have that problem with our divine inheritance. God's infinite, imperishable riches actually increase with the addition of each new heir, because part of the "wealth" is represented by the number of precious and priceless souls that join the kingdom. God has worked out a system in which we never come out on the short end of the deal. It's baffling, for sure.

The fact that we would receive anything at all from God is astounding in itself. The added fact that what we will receive is available in unlimited abundance is more than we can comprehend. But that's God's great mercy for you: abundant and incomprehensible.

Lord, I know I don't deserve to inherit a thing from you. I also know I don't deserve even to be considered an heir of anything in your kingdom. Thank you for accepting me into your family and keeping my inheritance in reserve for me in heaven.

75

A Permanent Register

He who overcomes will . . . be dressed in white. I will never blot out his name from the book of life, but will acknowledge his name before my Father and his angels.

Revelation 3:5

THIS passage addressed to the church in Sardis follows another familiar verse in Revelation: "Wake up! Strengthen what remains and is about to die, for I have not found your deeds complete in the sight of my God" (v. 2). The one who overcomes, mentioned in verse 5, is the person who awakens himself from his spiritual coma, strengthens the life that is left in him through repentance and obedience, and thus becomes worthy to walk with God.

That person's name will be written in the book of life, which means God will count him as a citizen of the Holy City, the New Jerusalem. In other words, he has placed his trust in Christ. By accepting the offer of salvation through Christ's work on the cross, the overcomer will hear his name when the roll is called up yonder.

Part of God's promise to this redeemed person is that he will never blot out his name from this book of life, unlike the original book of life that the Israelites kept. That book recorded all the names of the Israelites; when a person sinned, his name would be blotted out (Exod. 32:33). God knows what he's doing when he records your name, and he knows he will never change his mind about where you will spend eternity.

In addition, Christ will go to the Father and the angels and tell them all about you—about how you turned from your former way of life and became a Christ-follower. What that comes down to is this: Jesus Christ will vouch for you, always and forever.

There's also that bit about being dressed in white: soil-free, stain-free, sin-free white, a symbol of purity. God will clothe you in garments that tell the world that you are pure and holy in his sight. And that you, who are worthy, will have the distinct privilege of walking with him (v. 4).

How many more assurances can God give us? He tells us over and over again that we are his, that nothing will ever change that, that he wants us to live with him forever. He even writes our names in a permanent register, with indelible ink no less, promising never to erase them.

We owe him so much, and yet he has paid the price for us. But still, there is at least one thing we can do: acknowledge Christ before our friends and family, just as Christ acknowledges us before the Father and his angels.

———

Lord, I want my name to be permanently recorded in your book of life. Thank you for promising that you will always vouch for me, never remove my name from your register, and allow me to walk with you in purity and worthiness.

76

Getting to Know God

I will give them a heart to know me, that I am the LORD. They will be my people, and I will be their God, for they will return to me with all their heart.

Jeremiah 24:7

I T's so hard to get to know other people, with all the masks they wear, the roles they play, and the efforts they make to keep others from seeing who they really are inside.

It's also hard to get to know ourselves, with all the masks we wear, the roles we play, and the efforts we make to keep ourselves from seeing who we really are inside.

It's actually amazing that we ever get to know anyone at all—or that we even bother trying. Many of us have been burned by a relative, friend, or spouse; just when we thought we knew him, he hurt us by doing something we never thought he would. Just when we were ready to trust her, she turned into someone we never really knew.

And ourselves! We do everything under the sun to avoid spending time alone because we don't want to run the risk of exposing our true nature to ourselves.

With people, it can be like that.

But not with God. It's ironic: the more we get to know him, the more we realize how little we know him. But the more we get to know him, the more we learn to trust him. As our knowledge increases, so does our awareness of our ignorance. And yet, our trust deepens.

In Jeremiah 24:7 God declared that he would give his people a heart to know him. He even gives us the means—openness, trust, and acceptance. To not take advantage of this gift and this invitation is to waste a priceless opportunity.

Imagine if someone you admire were to make a similar opportunity available to you. Say you're a budding cellist, and Yo-Yo Ma makes you an offer you can't refuse: he welcomes you into his home and offers to share with you everything he knows about music, the cello, and greatness. Oh, and you can stay for as long as you like, all expenses paid. You'd be a fool not to take him up on the offer, right?

God's offer is much better, and yet so many of his people fail to take him up on it. Wouldn't you like to get to know God in a deeper and more meaningful way? You can, by spending time with him each day. God's offer comes loaded with guarantees for this life and the one to follow. You won't find that anywhere else.

———

Lord, I want to get to know you better. Thank you for giving me a heart that is able to respond to your incomparable invitation to increase my knowledge of you and your ways and to deepen my trust in you.

77

May It Go Well with You

"Honor your father and mother"—which is the first commandment with a promise—"that it may go well with you and that you may enjoy long life on the earth."

Ephesians 6:2–3

As Creator of the family, God considers relationships among family members to be of supreme importance. In fact, the first of the Ten Commandments that govern interpersonal relationships is the one that Paul quoted in these verses. God sees the family unit as foundational to the stability and security of society, and he wants his people to tread very carefully in and around that unit.

The Lord could have just as easily told Moses to start the fifth commandment with the words "Obey your mother and father . . ." But by using the word "honor," God placed emphasis on the heart attitude that motivates a person to follow through with right actions. Obedience to a boss or a prison guard—or a parent—whom you hate is rooted in coercion, not honor. If you base your actions on respect, your obedience flows naturally from that attitude.

At this point, the promise kicks in: "It may go well with you." *May everything go your way; may you find success, prosperity, and good health; may you have years of joy surrounded by loving family and good friends. Yes, may it go well with you.*

But what about the provision for a long life? We all have known people who honored their parents but died young. In this commandment, God's promise of a long life was tied to the land he had set aside for his people: "that you may live long in the land the LORD your God is giving you" (Exod. 20:12). Israel would occupy and inhabit the promised land for a long time if they secured the stability of their culture by honoring the family unit.

In Ephesians, Paul promised a long life, which may simply mean that God will bless you in a special way during your time on earth as long as you continue to have a favorable heart attitude toward your parents. And that applies to those whose parents are no longer alive. Maybe you failed to honor your parents before you came to know the Lord, and now that they are gone, you don't know what to make of this verse. Remember this: you still have the opportunity to honor the memory of your father and mother.

No matter how they were at parenting—no matter whether you even knew them or not—your parents gave you life. By honoring them, you honor God and acknowledge his work of grace in your life. Maybe the favor you bestow on your parents is unmerited, but it is, after all, a reflection of the unmerited favor God has bestowed on you.

———

Lord, show me how to honor my parents—for your sake. Help me to extend to them the grace you have shown me. If I live long and do well, so be it. If not, it makes no difference. I want only to please you by obeying your commands.

78

No Condemnation

Therefore, there is now no condemnation for those who are in Christ Jesus, because through Christ Jesus the law of the Spirit of life set me free from the law of sin and death.

Romans 8:1–2

MANY of us have no time to think about the prospect of God condemning us, because we spend so much time condemning ourselves. We set ourselves up as judge and jury over our own lives, and we find ourselves to be harsh and unforgiving, meting out the most severe punishment possible. Meanwhile, the real Judge, the only one whose decision matters, refuses to condemn us. We are a thickheaded lot at times.

When we accepted God's gracious offer of salvation through Jesus Christ, God forgave all of our sins—past, present, and future. Therefore God promised that he will never subject us to condemnation for them. We still need to confess our sins for our own sake, so that we can experience God's ongoing forgiveness. But he will never condemn us; that threat simply does not exist.

What God has condemned is sin itself; he has sentenced it to death in the lives of those who are "in Christ Jesus"—those who have taken on the life of Christ as their own. The Holy Spirit, the Spirit of life, sets you free from even the prospect of a judgment of "Guilty" (Rom. 8:1).

Your biggest challenge in seeing this promise fulfilled in your own life, then, may be the challenge to stop condemning yourself. A little imaginary exercise may help. Say you've been charged with, oh, a thousand counts of lewd and lascivious behavior in your thought life. Your only privilege in this particular courthouse of your mind is the freedom to choose which judge will hear your case. The presiding judge in courtroom A is a killer, the proverbial hanging judge. She's never been lenient, and she's got a personal grudge against you. She thinks you ought to be a much better person than you are. She should know; after all, she lives in your head.

The presiding judge in courtroom B is the one known as the God of all grace. Before you even have a chance to present your case, he pronounces you "Not guilty." "Sin? What sin?" he asks, as he looks over the docket placed before him. You have heard that he has refused to condemn anyone who bears the evidence of the Holy Spirit in her life. You just happen to have solid proof of that.

To allow the judge in courtroom A to hear your case would be tantamount to pleading insanity. So you walk right past that one and try to open the door to courtroom B. You can't, because it's locked. The Judge has dismissed the charges against you. It's all over; there is no need to assemble the court.

———

Lord, keep me from condemning myself when I sin—and even when I don't. You know what a harsh judge I can be. Remind me of your mercy and grace and the padlocked door to your courtroom. Thank you for dismissing the charges against me.

79

Simple Obedience

But I gave them this command: "Obey me, and I will be your God and you will be my people. Walk in all the ways I command you, that it may go well with you."

Jeremiah 7:23

At first glance, this promise in the Book of Jeremiah seems to be based on reward: obey God, and he will reward you for your obedience by making sure that all will go well for you. But read another way, the verse implies that the good life is a natural consequence of obeying God.

That certainly makes sense. If you were to live your life guided only by godly precepts—without a single moment of selfishness or questionable motivation—things would probably go well for you, wouldn't they? It would help, of course, if everyone else maintained the same level of obedience. But still, your obedience to God's guidance and direction would be a significant factor in improving the quality of the life you lead.

The Jews to whom God was speaking in this passage had so complicated their dealings with him that there was very little left that resembled relationship. Ritual, ceremony, and sacrifice had taken the place of pure and simple obedience. God reminded them of the simplicity that once characterized their communication with each other.

We should be better at maintaining an obedient relationship with God than the Israelites were, if for no other reason than that we have their example from which to learn. Moreover, we have the Spirit indwelling and empowering us to be obedient. But about all we've done is stop making sacrifices; no matter how free and easygoing a church may be, it still has its rituals and ceremonies to take the place of obedience.

We may never live to see this promise fulfilled, only because we may never learn the simple lessons of obedience that God has been trying to teach us since the first day we became his. We like to think that if we had been among the Israelites of Jeremiah's day, or among the first Jews who believed that Jesus was the Messiah, our obedience would have been pure and total. But our actions betray us; we find every excuse in the book and then some to justify our "inability" to obey. Only the Lord himself knows how we would respond if he ever expected us to obey him in the face of genuine persecution and retribution.

If things are not going well for us, we have only ourselves to blame. We simply have lost the will to obey.

————

Lord, make me an obedient person. Stop me whenever I try to come up with an excuse for not obeying you. I know that if I would just follow your lead, all would go well with me.

80

Forbidden Territory

So I say, live by the Spirit, and you will not gratify the desires of the sinful nature.

Galatians 5:16

IF anyone out there still believes that the sin of lust is a problem that plagues only unbelievers, that person is clearly out of touch with reality. Lust—which can describe any unhealthy desire—permeates the church. No one is immune to sinful longings; men and women, believers and unbelievers, old and young, churched and unchurched are all vulnerable to unholy attractions.

At one time, many people believed that they could escape the magnetic pull of sexual desire by avoiding places and activities where that desire might be strongest: at the beach, where bare skin was prevalent, at a dance where bodies actually made contact, or at a movie theater, where the titillating images on the screen could arouse errant responses. But there are at least two flaws in that way of thinking. One, it doesn't work anymore, if it ever did, because bare skin, bodies making contact, and titillating images are everywhere now; and two, because lust begins in the mind, not on the beach, at a dance, or in a movie theater. Your mind is always with you, and it needs precious little stimulation to venture into dangerous territory.

In his letter to the Galatians, Paul assured the faithful that it was possible to avoid gratifying the desires of their sinful nature. In Galatians 5:19, he clarified what those desires were; the first three he named were immorality, impurity, and sensuality. *If you live by the Spirit,* he told the church, *then you will not give in to those sins.*

If we have the Spirit indwelling us, aren't we living by the Spirit? And if that's the case, why do Spirit-indwelt believers succumb to sexual sin?

Living by the Spirit involves a conscious reordering of your life to conform to what God desires for you. It takes both a mind-set and a heart attitude that are continually turned toward God. When you live by the Spirit, your thoughts and actions are under the Spirit's influence, insuring that your mind and your heart will not consider going astray.

When you live by the Spirit, you become extrasensitive to those things that create an unhealthy response in you. The instant you become aware of any lustful thought, bring your mind back under the influence of the Spirit, thus insuring that your actions will be acceptable to God. The Spirit will never let you go anywhere unless your mind has gone there first.

———

Lord, thank you for sending the Holy Spirit to keep me from giving in to the lustful desires of my sinful nature. Help me to remember to bring my mind under the Spirit's influence as soon as my thoughts start to wander into dangerous and forbidden territory.

81

Anxiety-Free Living

Then Jesus said to his disciples, "Therefore I tell you, do not worry about your life, what you will eat; or about your body, what you will wear. Life is more than food, and the body more than clothes."

Luke 12:22–23

DON'T you think it would have been great to be one of Jesus' disciples? To have been in his presence while he was on Earth, to walk with him and talk with him and hang on his every word? Imagine how wonderful it was for the first disciples!

Now, shake off that fantasy image and think what it was *really* like for those twelve men. They had abandoned everything that represented a secure life. They experienced the reproach of their friends and families as well as the leaders of the dominant religious culture. They ran the risk of being cast out of the temple—denied the freedom to worship there—which meant Jewish society would turn its back on them.

The disciples had reason to worry. Sure, they believed Jesus would be their King someday, but still . . . things were not looking all that good.

Jesus knew what was in their hearts before they ever uttered a word, because he was well acquainted with human nature. He reminded them that life was more than the sum of its details. He challenged them to look at how God had provided for the rest of creation; how much more so would God provide for those he loved and who had chosen to follow his Son?

Now look at the reality of your own life. Each day brings with it countless reasons to worry, and not just about things like food and clothing. Will your son have the good sense not to get in a car with guys who have been drinking? Will your mother remember to take her blood pressure medication? Will your car make it to work today—and back home again? Will your supervisor ask for that report you were supposed to do yesterday?

Some circumstances in your life you have no control over at all; you can't always be with your son or your mother. Then there are circumstances over which you have some control; you would have gotten the car fixed if you'd had the money. And of course, there are those pesky circumstances over which you have complete control, like that report you didn't feel like finishing.

Show God how much you trust him by giving your worry and anxiety—all of it—to him. His love and concern for you extend even as far as that report that you failed to complete. Be anxious for *nothing*. You can trust him with everything.

———

Lord, I've come to see that worry is sin. I know that I can and must trust you to handle those things in life over which I have no control—as well as those things over which I do. Thank you for freeing me from the burden of anxiety.

82

Your Place in Heaven

And God raised us up with Christ and seated us with him in the heavenly realms in Christ Jesus, in order that in the coming ages he might show the incomparable riches of his grace, expressed in his kindness to us in Christ Jesus.

Ephesians 2:6–7

MANY of us are accustomed to singing those wonderful hymns and praise choruses about how great heaven will be. Heaven as a concept sounds, well, heavenly. But have you taken a look at the blueprint?

If you interpret Revelation 21 as a depiction of what heaven looks like—and the grand jury of biblical scholarship is still out on that—then you have to admit, it's an unusual place indeed. A bit intimidating, even.

Picture this: The walls are made of jasper; the streets are made of pure gold that looks like clear glass. Precious stones form the foundation of the city. Twelve enormous pearls form twelve gates to the city. Sounds like something out of a Jules Verne novel until you get to the part about light. The only illumination in the city: "The glory of God gives it light, and the Lamb is its lamp" (Rev. 21:23). Revelation also gives the angelic dimensions of the city, which John, the writer, assured us are identical to human dimensions. At least *something* will be familiar.

Maybe you can't wait to pass through those gates of pearl and take a stroll on those streets of gold. But even if you're among those who are somewhat unsure about this image of heaven, one thing is certain: it's going to be a grand and glorious place, because in heaven there will be no more mourning, crying, pain, or death, and because God himself will be there.

Your hope of heaven is not one to take lightly. Where you spend eternity is decided here on earth, not by Saint Peter or some angel standing at the gates, questioning you about your deeds on earth. No, you make the decision in the here and now about where you will spend the there and then. No angel, no saint who has preceded you to heaven will stand in judgment of you. When your time on earth is over, you will be ushered into the presence of God or banished from his presence forever.

Lay hold of the promise of heaven. Look forward to being seated with God in the heavenly realm. And each time you sing about it, let your imagination wander through the heavenly places. Just remember to keep in mind the main element in the blueprint: the image of Jesus, standing with his arms outstretched, waiting for you to collapse in his embrace. There's no better picture of heaven than that one.

———

Thank you, Lord, for preparing such an incredible place to spend eternity. No matter what heaven is like, I know that it will be a place of incomparable wonder, beauty, and majesty, because you will be there.

83

A Profound Peace

Peace I leave with you; my peace I give you. I do not give to you as the world gives. Do not let your hearts be troubled and do not be afraid.

John 14:27

Do you remember what life was like before you came to know Jesus? When you think of the way your life once was, you may tend to focus on what your lifestyle was like, and that may or may not have changed dramatically.

But one of the most profound changes in your life was probably one that took place on the inside, far from the eyes of curious on-lookers who were trying to figure out what this whole "religion thing" was about. That change was the *peace* that permeated your life.

Trying to describe this peace to someone who does not know Jesus is difficult, to understate the challenge. The peace Christ promises keeps us on an even keel when circumstances rock our world. It enables us to maintain our composure as our enemies throw their best stuff at us. The peace of Christ is a calming influence that no tranquilizer can rival.

If you have never known this peace, you are long overdue. The problem may be—well, no doubt *is*—of your own making, but you have a lot of company. When we fail to experience the peace of Christ, it's often because we have allowed ourselves to become so overburdened with anxiety that it rules our hearts and minds in place of Christ's peace.

David was apparently vulnerable to the disquieting effects of anxiety, but he knew where to find relief: "When anxiety was great within me," he wrote in Psalm 94:19, "your consolation brought joy to my soul." David turned to God, who utterly vanquished his fear. God restored not just peace but also joy to David's soul.

That kind of transformation can come only at the hand of God. You can exercise every bit of willpower within you, and you'll never be able to muster up the kind of peace and joy God gives. The peace of Christ is a natural result of living in close relationship and submission to him, allowing him to minister to you and allowing his peace to rule over your heart and mind.

Don't let your hearts become troubled, Jesus tells us. *Don't be afraid of anything. I've left my peace with you for you to enjoy.* Why suffer the painful and suffocating consequences of anxiety when Christ has offered the solution? Open your heart and your mind to his peace; allow the promise of his consolation to bring joy to your soul.

———

Lord, I never really knew what peace was until I came to know you. You have faithfully filled my heart and my mind with your peace under circumstances that would have caused me to unravel if I did not know you. I am so grateful to you for sharing your peace with me.

84

Prayer Offered in Faith

Is any one of you sick? He should call the elders of the church to pray over him and anoint him with oil in the name of the Lord. And the prayer offered in faith will make the sick person well; the Lord will raise him up. If he has sinned, he will be forgiven.

James 5:14–15

WHAT is the first thing you think to do when you get sick? It's probably *not* to call on the elders of your church to have them pray for you and anoint you with oil. If we all did that every time we fell ill, our elders would have a full-time prayer and anointing job.

Though there are occasions when it is advisable to call on the elders to perform this service, it's also good to know that the promise of healing is not always connected with a ritual involving others. What's important is the principle behind the promise—the principle that prayer for healing is effective. It's not the assembling of the elders or the administering of the oil that does the healing; they are symbolic gestures of agreement in prayer and the comforting presence of the Holy Spirit.

What brings about the healing, according to this verse, is the prayer offered in faith. Have you ever offered a prayer that was not "in faith"? Most people have. We want so much to believe in God's promises, and we try to pray accordingly. But deep down, we have our doubts. We have known too many people who were not healed. We have prayed too often and have not experienced healing for ourselves. We end up placing our faith in past failure.

We cannot understand why God heals one person and not another—or why he heals us from one illness but not another. Nor should we try to understand, because healing is a matter of God's sovereignty. Our responsibility is to do what God requires of us and leave the final decision to him. What he requires of us, of course, is faith, a deep and abiding trust that he will do what he has promised to do.

If you need healing or know someone who does, pray the Scriptures on healing back to God. For example, take the last part of Isaiah 53:5—"and by his wounds we are healed"—and speak it to God: "Lord, you have said in your Word that the beating Christ suffered on my behalf has healed me. I believe your Word and believe that I can walk in wholeness and health because of what Christ endured for my sake."

You can pray some verses verbatim, like Jeremiah 17:14: "Heal me, O Lord, and I will be healed." There are others that require a simple change in wording, like Psalm 103:1–3: "I praise you, Lord; my inmost being praises your holy name. I will not forget your benefits, Lord—you forgive all my sins and heal all my diseases." You can use other verses to remind God of his promise of healing or other instances of healing: "Lord, in Jeremiah 33:6 you say you will heal your people; I'm asking you to heal me" or "Lord, in Mark 5:34, you told a woman that her faith had healed her; I believe you can heal me as well."

Let God see that the prayer you offer is in faith. Believe that he will raise you up from the sickbed. As you wait in patient expectation for your healing to come, thank God for his many healing words.

———

Lord, I believe that the prayer offered in faith is enough to heal me. Let me always exercise both wisdom and faith when it comes to trusting you to heal me. I acknowledge your sovereignty as I wait in patient and faith-filled expectation for my healing to come.

85

Power for Service

It was he who gave some to be apostles, some to be prophets, some to be evangelists, and some to be pastors and teachers, to prepare God's people for works of service, so that the body of Christ might be built up.

Ephesians 4:11–12

A YOUNG evangelist once received several letters from his mentor in the ministry. He could hardly believe what his mentor, whom he had shadowed as they traveled together on the mission field, had written. Sensing that his days on earth were numbered, the older man was passing his mantle of ministry on to the younger man and encouraging him to face the future with fearlessness, power, love, and a sound mind.

Sound familiar? It should. That's what the apostle Paul wrote to his protégé in 2 Timothy 1:7. Reading between the lines of his letters, we can assume Paul was concerned about the younger evangelist's confidence that he could follow in Paul's footsteps. Indeed, taking up the apostle's ministry would be a daunting prospect. But Paul was certain that Timothy was equal to the task; all he needed to do was rekindle the gift for service that God had given him when

Paul laid hands on him. Paul's assessment was apparently accurate, as Timothy went on to lead the church as one of its earliest bishops.

Timothy's training for service came from Paul, but his power for service did not. That came from God. Paul needed to remind Timothy of this, so that when he departed from this world Timothy would have no reason to fear that his effectiveness would diminish.

The power that was available to Timothy in the first century is also available to you today. If God has called you to serve him—and if you are a believer, rest assured, he has—he promises to equip and empower you to fulfill whatever act of service he has called you to do. You can be certain that if he has called you to teach, he will equip you to teach; if he called you to evangelize, he will equip you to evangelize. Likewise for those he calls to be pastors and prophets and so forth; he will never call you to a ministry he will not equip you to perform.

You may have serious doubts about your own abilities. You may think you're not able to fulfill the obligations of the ministry to which he has called you. You may think all kinds of negative thoughts about you and your abilities, but your self-assessment does not matter one bit. All that matters is God's call and his promise to empower you to fulfill the requirements of that call. Forget your own analysis, and remember his promise.

———

Lord, thank you for promising to make me able to accomplish the work you have called me to do. Help me to ignore my own lack of confidence and to place my hope in you alone. I know that with you, I can accomplish anything that is within your will.

86

Strength in Numbers

Again, I tell you that if two of you agree on earth about anything you ask for, it will be done for you by my Father in heaven. For where two or three come together in my name, there am I with them.

Matthew 18:19–20

FOR the Jewish audience to whom Jesus spoke these words, the Lord's promise represented another break with religious tradition. Jewish tradition prevented any religious assembly unless a *minyan*—a quorum of ten men—was present. Here Jesus told his followers that such a quorum was unnecessary, with regard to both the gender and the minimum number of participants.

Agreement, of course, requires two people, so the number of participants would apply in that case. But by not restricting the participants to men, Jesus was once again ruffling the feathers of the leaders of the dominant religious culture, something he did with amazing regularity.

Even today, some religious leaders feel threatened when "two or three" gather outside the four walls of the church to pray or study the Bible together; the notion of an elite class of Bible scholars who alone know the truth just doesn't seem ever to go away completely. Disregard the paranoia of the exclusivists and trust God to lead you and your assembled little band of believers into all truth. It's comforting to know that when we come together in the Lord's name, he promises to be there with us. We don't need to always be in a church building with hundreds or thousands of other believers to experience the presence of the Lord.

What's more, it's humbling to think of the power he gives us when even a small number of believers agree in prayer on a particular matter. But don't we have power in prayer when we pray on our own, tucked away in our isolated prayer closets? Yes, but there's a decent chance that what the Lord was encouraging here was cooperation among his followers. Getting two or three people to agree on anything can be a monumental task at times, and it's probably fair to assume that Jesus wanted God's people to discover how essential it is for them to work together for the common good. Nothing less than the ultimate goal, the ushering in of the kingdom of God, was at stake.

Welcome the Lord into your presence whenever you gather in his name with two or three other believers. Agree on what to ask him for in prayer, and then pray, believing that your Father in heaven will do what you ask. And never forget the awesome power he has entrusted to you. Remain humbled by that power, and you will never abuse it.

———

Lord, teach me to cooperate with my fellow believers, reminding me always of how pleasing it is to you when we agree with each other and work together to bring your kingdom to pass. Thank you not only for promising to answer our prayers of agreement but also for promising to be right there in the midst of our gathering.

87

Purpose of God's Word

So is my word that goes out from my mouth:
It will not return to me empty,
but will accomplish what I desire
and achieve the purpose for which I sent it.

Isaiah 55:11

Pick a promise—any promise. You can be assured that it will come to pass, if on no other basis than the word of the Lord spoken through the prophet Isaiah. Every word that proceeds from his mouth, he says, will echo its truth down through the ages. And that echo will not return to God empty; it will return full of accomplishment, achievement, and purpose.

To appreciate this promise, we need to know what God has said. It's all there in the Bible, so getting to know that book is critical. The Bible, of course, is the best-selling volume of all time. But it's not necessarily the most frequently read. Many people find the sheer size of the Bible to be daunting; others have no idea where to start; still others start strong on a Bible reading program but soon give up on it.

God actually made his Word far more accessible than we realize.

The beauty of the Scriptures—aside from the inherent truth they embody, that is—is that you can read them any number of ways, all of them profitable and valid.

Following a reading plan—available in many Bibles and from numerous ministries—is helpful for people who prefer an established schedule. You can also start with a book that is especially appealing to you, such as Psalms or the Gospel of John. And there's nothing wrong with skipping around, reading a little here and a little there, once you get your bearings and you know where here and there are.

Regardless of how you read God's Word, you can expect to come away with new insights each time you open your Bible. Familiar verses can suddenly seem fresh and full of meaning that you never saw before. That's the Holy Spirit at work in your life, teaching you and interpreting God's Word for you. As always, God has not left you on your own to sort all this out.

God's promise is that the time you spend reading your Bible is never wasted. You will never exhaust its riches; you will never get to a point where it has nothing more to teach you; you will never reach the end of it, no matter how many times you read straight through to Revelation 22:21, the last verse. And you will never find its promises to be empty. They will always accomplish the purpose God intended.

———

Lord, I know I could spend more time in your Word than I do. It has ministered to me so much in the past, and I know it will continue to for the rest of my life. Keep nudging me with reminders to open my Bible and allow the Holy Spirit to reveal its truth to me. Thank you, Lord, for providing such a treasure for your people.

88

Strength for the Journey

Even youths grow tired and weary,
and young men stumble and fall;
but those who hope in the LORD
will renew their strength.
They will soar on wings like eagles;
they will run and not grow weary,
they will walk and not be faint.

Isaiah 40:30–31

I F you haven't visited a gym lately, you might be surprised to see who is working out on the weight machines right next to all those buff young bodies in the advertisements. In gyms around the country, older Americans are learning that they can renew their physical strength in an astonishingly short amount of time.

God's promise in Isaiah 40 is even better. Those hardy young bodies, Isaiah wrote, don't stand a chance if their hope is not in the Lord. They'll just end up tired and weary, and stumbling and falling all over the place. But those who hope in the Lord—young and old alike—will find supernatural strength for their journeys through life.

Maybe you're feeling a bit faint along about now. You've been walking with the Lord for a number of years, and you haven't stopped to refresh yourself for some time. God says you *can* renew your own strength, as long as you have not lost sight of the hope you have in him.

Wouldn't you like to soar on the wings of an eagle? If you've ever watched an eagle in flight, you know what a glorious sight that is. Spiritually, you can fly as effortlessly as an eagle, drawing your strength from the one who soars above all.

Wouldn't you also like to run and not grow weary? Think of the marathons you could win! Well, life is a marathon, at times consisting of a variety of dashes and sprints. You *can* run a spiritual marathon without ever growing weary, as long as you keep your eyes on the one who goes before you.

Finally, wouldn't you love to walk and not be faint? You could hike the Appalachian Trail in record time, or take in the breathtaking beauty of the Pacific Coast without the distraction of fatigue. You *can* take a trek through your life of faith without feeling faint, as long as you follow in the footprints of the one who goes before you.

Next time you're at the gym, think about how much better God's promises are than those of the gym's ads. Older people may restore their physical strength through weight training and younger people may be able to maintain their strong bodies, but those who hope in the Lord have a much better prospect for a healthy future. Their hope for the future includes soaring and running and walking, with a renewed, supernatural strength.

———

Lord, I want to soar with eagles and run a marathon and walk forever, without losing my spiritual strength. Keep my eyes focused steadily on you. Teach me how to draw on your energy—and keep reminding me that as long as I depend on you to refresh me, my age does not matter at all.

89

To Be Young Again

[He] satisfies your desires with good things
so that your youth is renewed like the eagle's.

Psalm 103:5

REMEMBER the last time you felt like a kid? You were probably doing something that made you feel carefree, joyous, and playful. It may surprise you to know that amid all the seriousness of the Bible, with its life-and-death, where-will-you-spend-eternity decisions, God injects a verse here and there that shows he wants you to feel like a kid once again.

Isaiah 55:12—"You will go out in joy and be led forth in peace; the mountains and hills will burst into song before you, and all the trees of the field will clap their hands"—is but one of those verses. Here's another: "But for you who fear My name the sun of righteousness will rise with healing in its wings; and you will go forth and skip about like calves from the stall" (Mal. 4:2 NASB). And another: "Then will the lame leap like a deer, and the tongue of the dumb shout for joy. Water will gush forth in the wilderness and streams in the desert" (Isa. 35:6). And yet another: "And all the people went up after him, playing flutes and rejoicing greatly, so that the ground shook with the sound" (1 Kings 1:40). These are not exactly the images you're likely to impose on an austere, grim-faced professional Christian.

Forget about Botox and plastic surgery. Looking young is nothing compared to youthfulness that God has renewed. He knows what aging feels like, and he knows how to make you feel young again. Ask anyone who has found his purpose in life at an advanced age; suddenly, his energy soars, and he can do things he hasn't even attempted for decades. Purpose is one of those good things that God gives you, and it will restore your youth like nothing else can.

God's purpose for your life will always make the most of your natural talents and the special gifts he has given you. Using those talents and gifts in God's service will keep you from believing your life counts for nothing, that you are no longer a useful and productive member of either society or the church. And it keeps you energetic, because you simply can't keep going for God unless you have the energy to keep going at all.

A high energy level, though, is just one of the physical characteristics we often associate with the young. Two others are speed and strength, which are also characteristic of eagles. That's what God wants you to feel like: a strong eagle streaking through the air. It's the freedom of flight, the ability to soar above the cares of the world, the stamina to endure a long journey that he wants you to experience.

Let God know what your desires are, and watch him satisfy them with the good things from his storehouse. And then watch as you undergo a serious makeover, one that will restore your high-energy youthfulness once again.

———

Lord, thank you for giving me a purpose for my life. Any time I am actively involved in serving you in a way that conforms to the purpose you have for me, I know what it's like to feel young again. Thank you, too, for understanding us so well that you recognize our need to have our youthfulness restored.

90

Sharing in Christ's Resurrection

And if the Spirit of him who raised Jesus from the dead is living in you, he who raised Christ from the dead will also give life to your mortal bodies through his Spirit, who lives in you.

Romans 8:11

THEOLOGIANS go round and round about what the resurrection of believers will look like. It's not as if we have some real-life example of a human resurrection to use as a model. Or do we?

When Jesus lived on earth, he was God in human form. As he suffered a slow death on the cross, he was God in human form. And when he rose from the grave, he was God . . . in transformed human form. He had a body that his followers could see and touch (Luke 24:36–43; John 20:26–28).

According to the Bible, we will share in Christ's resurrection. The Holy Spirit will "quicken," or give life to, our transformed human bodies when God raises us from the dead. What exactly will those bodies look like? That's where it gets theologically complicated and where we should probably stop our relentless curiosity and conjecturing. We don't know for sure. What we do know is that the disciples recognized the resurrected Jesus, who walked and talked and ate with them as always.

What we also know for sure is that the day of our bodily resurrection will be a glorious one indeed. Whatever form our bodies take, we know that they will be healed of all disease, restored, repaired, renewed, remodeled, completely overhauled—you name it. No fashion magazine makeover—those temporary transformations that take all day, thousands of dollars, and a cast of professionals to accomplish—can compare with the instantaneous and permanent makeover you'll get on resurrection day. Save your time and your money; your day is coming.

But until the day when you will experience your own bodily resurrection, you can rejoice in the knowledge that the Holy Spirit breathes life into your body right now. Through his indwelling presence, you already share in the life of Christ; through his life-giving power, you will share in the life of the resurrected Christ. The promise of Romans 8:11 is for both now and then, as long as the Spirit of him who raised Jesus from the dead is living in you. As long as you have that matter covered, you've got the rest of the verse covered as well.

———

Lord, I don't need to understand everything about the bodily resurrection to come. I can wait until then to find out the details. Right now, I am so grateful to you for allowing me to share in your resurrection and spend eternity with you. I rejoice in the knowledge that even now, the Spirit is breathing spiritual life into this mortal body you have given me. Thank you for the body you have given me now and the one you will give me in the future.

91

Praise from God

Therefore judge nothing before the appointed time; wait till the Lord comes. He will bring to light what is hidden in darkness and will expose the motives of men's hearts. At that time each will receive his praise from God.

1 Corinthians 4:5

IN the section preceding this portion of Paul's first letter to the church at Corinth, the apostle chided the Corinthian believers for their immature behavior, particularly with regard to boasting about their accomplishments. This, Paul said, was foolish behavior and counterproductive to the spread of the gospel. As God's fellow workers, Christians are responsible for cooperating with each other in the tremendous challenges they face; failure to cooperate distracts attention from where it belongs—on the Spirit of God, who does the real work.

And furthermore—you can almost hear Paul trying to restrain himself—we do not have the right to judge others or even our own selves. "I care very little if I am judged by you or by any human court; indeed, I do not even judge myself. . . . It is the Lord who judges me," he wrote in verses 3 and 4, clearly implying that everyone should think about this the way he did. Then we get to the good part.

Admittedly, the part about the Lord bringing certain things to light sounds a bit ominous, but surely what is hidden in darkness includes an anonymous good deed or two, and some of our unexposed motives must border on the decent. In any event, God will one day turn the tables on us: *he* will be the one praising *us.*

Imagine what that will feel like. But first, resist the urge to focus on how short you think your particular praise-from-God time will be. See yourself standing before the Creator of the universe. Hear his powerful but tender voice praising you for all of those good things you did that you thought no one noticed—things that you had forgotten about long ago, things you may not even remember once God brings them up. Now resist the urge to deny that you ever could have been so thoughtful or that your motives ever could have been so pure. God knows what he's talking about; simply put, he's right and you're wrong. Be quiet and enjoy his praise.

You don't need the praise of others. You don't need to boast about your own accomplishments, and you certainly don't need to run other people down to make yourself look better. Just wait—wait until you hear the words of praise that God has stored up for you. His voice is the one worth listening for.

———

Lord, I cannot imagine that you will have any words of praise for me, but I'm willing to believe that you will. I look forward to the day when you expose those parts of my nature—the good ones—that I'm not even aware of.

92

Safe from Evil

The Lord will rescue me from every evil attack and will bring me safely to his heavenly kingdom. To him be glory for ever and ever. Amen.

2 Timothy 4:18

PAUL was one persecuted apostle. He seemed to have had a knack for stirring up trouble, without really trying. It wasn't as if he set out to be a problem child of God; he just spoke with such confidence, authority, and power that he upset people.

Toward the end of his second epistle to Timothy, he named his latest persecutor, some poor metalworker named Alexander whom the Bible mentions because of the harm he inflicted on Paul (1 Tim. 4:14–15). This guy was so opposed to Paul's message of salvation that the apostle warned Timothy to watch out for him as well.

While this verse may appear to be an assurance of safety on earth and security in heaven appropriate for Paul alone, that's apparently not what he intended to convey. Both letters to Timothy imply an underlying concern for Timothy's ability to carry on Paul's work. In writing this to his young friend, the older apostle was saying this: *Look, Timothy, we all come under attack. But God will rescue us from every single attack that we suffer, and he will make sure that each one of us arrives safely in his kingdom. He will not allow the evil one to snatch us out of his grasp.*

Satan orchestrates every attack brought against you, and he designs them to wear you down. He wants more than anything to weaken your spiritual resolve by hammering away at your commitment to Christ. He'll use anyone—your spouse, your children, your closest friends, your coworkers, and especially your brothers and sisters in Christ—to create emotional havoc and inflict gut-wrenching pain on your life. He did it to Paul, he probably did it to Timothy, and it's a good guess that he's done it to you. He keeps at it until he's got you on the mat.

But look up. There's God, holding out his strong arms to rescue you from Satan's clutches. Just when Satan thinks you're so weak that you'll gladly take him up on whatever he offers, God tightens his hold on you. He will never let Satan get his hands on you. He will never let go of you.

And because he promises to bring you safely into his kingdom, then to him be the glory forever and ever. We should do nothing less than praise him and exalt him as long as we have the breath to do so.

———

Lord, I know that I may never understand what it means to be severely persecuted for my faith in you. I can only hope and pray that I will stand strong in the face of whatever opposition I come up against throughout the rest of my life. Thank you for keeping me safe from the clutches of Satan.

93

Salvation of Your Family

Believe in the Lord Jesus, and you will be saved—you and your household.

Acts 16:31

THE whole episode started when Paul and Silas decided it was time to free a female slave from a demonic spirit. That didn't go over very well with her owners, who earned their living from her reputation as a fortune-teller. So they got Paul and Silas beaten and thrown into jail, not knowing that an earthquake would strike that very night and open the doors of the jail. The guard was then in full suicide mode, thinking the prisoners had escaped and he'd be killed anyway for letting them go.

But being good witnesses for God, Paul and Silas stayed put. Their obedience paid off. Overcome by mercy, the guard asked what he must do to be saved. Acts 16:31 records the answer.

We get the first part. If you believe in the Lord Jesus, you will be saved. But what about those last two words—"your household"? Did that mean that the guard's conversion would apply to his household—his family and his servants, if he had any—as well? No, and that's not how the promise applies to us today either. Nothing in Scripture even hints at the notion that one person's salvation can automatically be conferred on another. Each person must come to faith in Christ individually.

But one of the evidences of the Holy Spirit's powerful activity in the early church was the phenomenon of entire families being saved at one time. Scripture records three such events like the one that affected the guard's household: the conversion of Cornelius in Acts 10 and 11; Lydia earlier in Acts 16; and Crispus in Acts 18. And household conversions were not limited to first-century spiritual activity; they've been a part of the Spirit's work all along.

Even if your family didn't come to Christ as a cohesive unit, you have plenty of reason to believe that each family member will experience salvation. Despite the initial rejection, despite the derision, mocking, or whatever negative vibes your family has expressed toward your faith, the presence of even one believer has a powerful impact on the entire household.

You can trust God with your family. He wants them to come to faith in Christ more than you do. With you in their midst, they already have the Holy Spirit living among them, because he indwells you. That means that every day, they come face-to-face with the truth of the gospel. And you don't even have to say a word about it.

———

Lord, I want to believe that my entire family will be saved, but sometimes it's so hard. Remind me, when I fail to see any evidence of their hearts softening toward you, that you alone can see what is really going on inside them. And keep reminding me that the mere fact of my presence in the household exposes them to the truth about you.

94

The Second Coming of Christ

"Men of Galilee," they said, "why do you stand here looking into the sky? This same Jesus, who has been taken from you into heaven, will come back in the same way you have seen him go into heaven."

Acts 1:11

Probably no words comforted the disciples more than these: "This same Jesus . . . will come back." Jesus, the one they had seen die on a disgraced sinner's cross, the one whose body lay for three days in a cold, dark tomb, the one who came back from the dead only to leave them again—this one would come back. They had seen so many miracles, so many wonders. How could they fail to believe that Jesus would return to them?

By this time, the disciples had found their strength in the risen Christ. Even Peter, once scared and pitiful, had made an about-turn. He took command of Jesus' band of followers after Pentecost, speaking with a boldness that probably surprised even him (Acts 1:15–22; 2:14–40; 3:12–26; 4:8–12). And he never looked back, only ahead—to the certain return of his Lord and Master.

Believers down through the centuries have looked for Christ's return in their own time. Is this the time? Will ours be the generation that witnesses Christ returning to earth in clouds of glory? People have interpreted the signs and wonders of their times as providing unmistakable proof that theirs was the generation that would experience Christ's second coming.

And so far, every generation has been wrong.

Ultimately, it does not matter when Christ returns. It matters only that we as believers realize that *this* could be the year, the day, the hour that Christ chooses to come back to earth.

Unbelievers, of course, may mock you for that sense of urgency, that passion for evangelism that intensifies whenever you realize that the time may be short. Scoffers point to countless times that believers have incorrectly prophesied the return of Christ. False prophecy aside, what they fail to recognize is that it is God himself who places that drive to evangelize within you. He wants all to come to repentance and salvation, and he keeps his people from becoming lazy precisely by not telling them when Christ will return.

The fact that Jesus has not yet come back is evidence of God's patient nature and all-encompassing love. He wants to give those who hate, revile, scoff at, and blaspheme him every opportunity to embrace all that he has for them. He delays the second coming of Christ out of his kindness, compassion, and mercy toward all people.

Keep that sense of urgency about you. Continue to share the gospel of Jesus Christ as you look toward his eventual return. He promised to come back. *Will ours be the generation . . . ?*

Lord, I eagerly await your return, but I pray that I will not become lazy in the meantime. Keep that sense of urgency burning within me, despite the scoffers and the mockers. I ask that you would turn their hearts toward you.

95

Sleeping in Heavenly Peace

I will lie down and sleep in peace,
for you alone, O LORD,
make me dwell in safety.

Psalm 4:8

WITH all the sleep aids on the market, you would think that insomnia was a relatively recent problem. Not so; the Bible even records a number of occasions on which this king or that king was so troubled in his spirit about the problems in his realm that he was unable to sleep (Esther 6:1, for example).

But insomnia is a big enough problem in America for the major pharmaceutical companies to invest their research and development dollars into remedies for sleep disorders. Estimates on the number of Americans who suffer from chronic insomnia vary wildly, depending on who is dispensing the information and what his or her financial stake is in issuing high estimates. Let's just say that "millions" of Americans have trouble sleeping on a regular basis.

King David had as good a reason as any of our contemporaries for finding it difficult to fall asleep. He was beset by the constant attacks of his enemies, which all too often were also his relatives. And then there was the whole ugly mess with Bathsheba. It's a wonder the man ever got a good night's sleep. We know from the Psalms that there were nights when he didn't (Ps. 6:6, 63:6).

But on those nights when his thoughts and his heart were turned toward God, David found the peaceful sleep that eluded him at other times. He poured out his heart to God, handed him his worries and concerns, and expressed confidence in "you alone, O LORD," the only one who could ever promise that David would dwell in safety as he lay down and slept in peace.

There's a lesson here for us today. Instead of resorting to artificial sleep aids, we can rely on the supernatural power of the Holy Spirit to give us the peaceful sleep we so desperately need. Our lives *are* filled with stressors, even if our enemies don't exist in the form of marauding armies and power-hungry sons—or envious types like King Saul who see us as a threat. You know those things that cause anxiety in your life, and you know how they can interfere with your well-being. Identify your adversaries and turn them over, one by one, to the Lord each night. You can trust him to give you peaceful sleep.

David was blissfully unaware of the medical advances to come; we might want to revert to that blissfully ignorant condition ourselves. And if our newfound sleep aid—the comforting presence of the Holy Spirit—becomes habit-forming, all the better.

Lord, the peaceful sleep that you give me is such a blessing. I thank you for all those nights when you have calmed my disturbed spirit and quieted my unsettled mind. I know that I can turn to you with the confidence that you will take from me the worries of my day so that I may experience your peace.

96

Authority over the Enemy

I have given you authority to trample on snakes and scorpions and to overcome all the power of the enemy; nothing will harm you.

Luke 10:19

COMEDIAN Flip Wilson was the entertainer who popularized the saying "The devil made me do it." Wilson's comedic timing and delivery turned a spiritual reality into a standing joke on late-night talk shows. But it's no longer funny. The truth that Satan and his minions are up to no good in our lives has become an everyday reality for the people of God.

There's nothing amusing about the measures our unseen enemy will take to try to undo us. The disciples probably had little understanding of Satan's machinations as they listened to Jesus explain the spiritual authority they possessed. But their understanding would grow after Jesus' ascension, when the enemy turned his attention away from Christ and onto the disciples. He wanted to conquer them, the sooner the better.

Maybe the disciples got hung up on the image of snakes and scorpions. We're like that, too: we'll grab on to a concept that is tangible and completely miss the larger point. As the disciples may have done, we silently thank God for his protection from creepy crawlies and fail to recognize that Jesus was talking about dangers in the spirit world. The context in which this promise of protection and authority appears is entirely spiritual in nature.

Maybe we just don't want to think about dealing with demons. The spirit world may seem so frightening—or so unreal—that we'd rather come up against a venomous snake or a deadly scorpion. At least, we figure, we'd stand a chance against an earthly threat.

The truth is that we stand the ultimate chance against the spirit world, because Jesus assured us that he has passed along his spiritual authority to those who believe in him. He has given us not only the power to withstand the enemy's assault but also to overcome it. "Nothing will harm you," Jesus says, as we cower in a corner afraid of our own shadow.

What could possibly come against us and vanquish us when we have the authority of Christ at our command? Jesus has already conquered Satan and all the lesser powers in the demonic world. We know who the stronger power is, and we're on his side of the battle line. What more evidence could we possibly need? We have complete spiritual authority over the forces of evil—no doubt about it. The devil can't make us do a thing, nor can he touch us with his cruel intentions.

———

Lord, I claim the authority you have given me over Satan and his demonic minions. I know that I can fearlessly face whatever tactics they use to try to undo me. Through you, I will overcome them, and no harm will come to me. Thank you for passing along your power.

97

The Body and the Blood

Then Jesus declared, "I am the bread of life. He who comes to me will never go hungry, and he who believes in me will never be thirsty."

John 6:35

*N*OW this *is just too much. It was bad enough when this alleged prophet began creating all kinds of havoc among the fishermen of the area, getting them to ignore their work and follow him as he traipsed all over the countryside. But he seemed harmless enough until today—all that talk about eating his flesh and drinking his blood! I walked away from him, and I will never go back.*

That's pretty much what happened after Jesus answered the crowd's question about manna, the "bread of heaven," that God provided for the Israelites as they wandered in the desert (John 6:30–31). They didn't get it at first, so Jesus offered an explanation: "I am the bread of life," he said in John 6:35. "I am the bread that came down from heaven," he said in verse 41, making the Jewish leaders very, very angry.

But he didn't stop there. "This bread is my flesh" (v. 51). And finally, the clincher: "Unless you eat the flesh of the Son of Man and drink his blood, you have no life in you" (v. 53). Remember—these people did not have the Eucharist as a frame of reference. You've got to admit, this teaching would have been hard to take. In fact, it was so hard that many of Jesus' followers turned away from him (v. 66).

It's much easier for us today. As we celebrate Communion and partake of the body and the blood, Jesus' teaching comes to life for us. But even apart from the Eucharist, Jesus' words in John 6:35 have profound meaning for the ones who follow him.

Jesus promises that those who come to him and believe in him will never hunger or thirst—because his "food" and "drink" provide spiritual fullness, a spirit that is satisfied and content and full to overflowing with the richness of the treasures of God's wisdom. Those who embrace him and his teachings have found what they have been seeking all their lives: the answers, the hope, and the ful-fillment of the yearnings hidden deep within their spirits.

If you've ever experienced an empty spiritual life—and we all have, before we came to know Jesus—you know how miserable that can feel. You go through the motions of religious ritual, you look here and there for the answer to your relentless questions and long-ings, or you try to ignore your spiritual nature altogether. But noth-ing works. You need the Bread of Life, and you need him now. Only he can satisfy that hunger and thirst that torment you. Take what he offers—and never look back.

———

Lord, I want the bread and drink that you offer. When I partake of all that you are, you fill me to overflowing with spiritual blessings beyond measure. Thank you for offering yourself to me, so that I need not experience hunger or thirst for the things of the Spirit ever again.

98

Let There Be Light

I have come into the world as a light, so that no one who believes in me should stay in darkness.

John 12:46

D ARKNESS—the very word can send shivers up and down the spines of some people. Children, of course, don't take kindly to darkness, which they imagine hides all kinds of monsters, wild animals, spiders, and such. But even some adults find that they need to sleep with a light on now and then, as unusual sounds coming from both outside and inside the house give them reason to believe danger is afoot. Darkness can fill our minds with terror; for the most part, it is not our friend.

In the Bible, darkness represents at least two other realities in addition to terror: chaos and evil. In the beginning, before God uttered those precious four words—"Let there be light!"—all that existed was darkness. By creating light, God began the process of establishing order.

Darkness is associated with chaos, confusion, and disorder, especially in Hollywood depictions of catastrophes that knock out all artificial light—usually at the stroke of midnight. Or maybe in your own basement, as the darker nooks and crannies fill up with a confusion of boxes and bins full of stuff you've long ago forgotten about.

Throughout the Bible, darkness is also associated with evil. But it is not the same as the darkness associated with fear, because many people are actually drawn to evil. The Bible makes it clear that some people prefer to indulge in evil practices; they don't reluctantly give in to wickedness but fully embrace it. But they're often forced to do so under cover of . . . darkness, naturally. Their evil may take the form of practices that strike terror in the hearts of others, but they feel no fear—or so they say. The association of darkness with sin has lasted down through the centuries. There's little likelihood that we will ever think evil connotes light.

And that, of course, is because God is light. No darkness of chaos, terror, or evil can survive the light of God. His light brings order to our lives, drives away our fears, and draws us to a life of righteousness as we allow the radiance of Jesus to shine from within us. After all, he promised.

As long as you follow Jesus, no form of darkness can threaten you. The God who in the beginning said, "Let there be light!" is the same God who today says, "Let there be light in your life!" His light will never dim, never burn out, never go away.

Lord, there are so many ways in which you have become a light to me. I know what it was like to live in darkness, and I know what it is like to live in your glory. There is no contest between the two. I choose to live in your light forever.

99

Even Greater Things

I tell you the truth, anyone who has faith in me will do what I have been doing. He will do even greater things than these, because I am going to the Father.

John 14:12

HEALING the sick, restoring sight to the blind, causing the paralyzed to walk again, raising the dead? *What?* The disciples must have wondered: *Is Jesus really saying we will be able to do all these things once he goes to the Father, whatever that means? Does he really expect us to believe that?*

Well, we don't know how Jesus expected the disciples to react to his words, but we do know that we can stand on his promises. And we know that "signs and wonders"—miraculous healings, restorations, and even resurrections, in the name of Christ—have been recorded and verified countless times over the last two thousand years.

Skeptics aren't so sure. If this promise holds true, they ask, then why don't we witness those things, and even greater things, happening on a daily basis in what is supposed to be a "Christian" country? After giving them a short lesson on the truth that only individuals, and not nations, can be Christian, we get to the main point: that the promise is for anyone who has faith in Christ. That faith must be single-minded and unwavering, as James wrote in his epistle (1:7).

Furthermore, what Jesus meant by "greater things than these" is certainly subject to interpretation. Who's to say what is more important from God's perspective: a person raised from the dead or a person released from a lifetime of bondage to pornography? We may already be accomplishing a host of greater works without even realizing it—which may be exactly what God had planned for us all along.

Jesus' promise is for spiritual power, whatever form that may take. In your life, in your family, in your neighborhood, that may look a whole lot different from what it looks like in someone else's environment. He gives *you* the power to perform the spiritual works he has given *you* to accomplish.

Looking to what others are doing right now or what others have done in the past is pointless and distracting. God has a specific purpose for your life, and he promises to empower you to bring that purpose to fulfillment. Have enough faith in him to believe that you can do what he did while he was on earth—whether that means raising the dead or showing kindness and compassion to those who suffered abuse and abandonment by the dominant culture of his time. Both works are great in his sight.

———

Thank you, Lord, for giving me a purpose and the power to accomplish it. Keep me looking steadily at you instead of looking enviously at the great and mighty works that I see others doing. Remind me that "greater than these" can simply come down to doing what you have asked me to do.

100

The Breath of the Almighty

But it is the spirit in a man,
the breath of the Almighty,
that gives him understanding.

Job 32:8

THE breath of the Almighty! What a wonderful image! It was the breath of the Almighty that gave life to Adam (Gen. 2:7) and enabled humankind to understand—to perceive things beyond the obvious, to have insight into the underlying meaning behind what our five senses can access. To have understanding is to have the ability to make distinctions, use knowledge correctly, and "see" truth through spiritual perception.

True understanding, the kind the Bible encourages us to seek out and learn from, comes only from God himself. He is the one who created and understands all things; to seek wisdom from another source is to act foolishly and risk serious *mis*understanding. "Lean not on your own understanding," Proverbs 3:5 tells us, and with good reason. Ours is incomplete. God alone can provide complete understanding.

Your ability to understand the things of the Spirit is directly tied in with your willingness to seek insight from God. He will give you what you seek, because he breathed life into you so you *could* understand.

As with all of God's promises, the first step toward seeing the promise of understanding fulfilled in your life is to pray. Ask God for it. Open your heart and your mind to him; let go of your preconceived ideas. Acknowledge your faulty and incomplete comprehension of the underlying meanings behind those things you can perceive with your five senses.

Be specific with God; if you need a clearer understanding of a spiritual concept like salvation, tell him. He'll gladly accommodate you. Look at the kind of understanding God gave Daniel and his friends—knowledge and understanding about literature and "learning" and, in Daniel's case, about dreams and visions (Dan. 1:17). King Nebuchadnezzar grilled Daniel, Hananiah, Mishael, and Azariah about "every matter of wisdom and understanding" and found their answers to be ten times better than any he'd heard before (Dan. 1:20). If God was willing to educate those four young men in the field of literature, he's willing to answer your questions as well.

Nothing is beyond God's scope, so whatever it is you want to understand better, take your questions to him. He wants his people to have knowledge about all the mysteries of life. He wants you to bring your confusion, your limited human comprehension, and your desire for greater insight to him. Who knows? One day, your understanding of the deepest issues of life may be ten times better than what anyone has heard before.

———

Lord, I want to lean on your understanding and not my own. I know that you've given me insight into things that are far beyond my human ability to comprehend, and I am so thankful to you for that. Keep me looking to you as my source of all understanding.

101

Unified but Not Uniform

There is one body and one Spirit—just as you were called to one hope when you were called—one Lord, one faith, one baptism; one God and Father of all, who is over all and through all and in all.

Ephesians 4:4–6

UNITY among believers was such an important issue for Paul that he repeatedly reminded the churches he oversaw to immediately deal with dissension in the ranks. And as in these verses, he never missed an opportunity to hammer home the message of harmony in his letters.

However difficult it was for him to get the early church to act in one accord, his task almost seems easy compared to the monumental challenges we face today. Some believe that nothing less than a full-scale assault on our faith will get various factions in the church to find common ground, and even then it's not clear with which side some Christian sects would align themselves! In many cases, a minor doctrine—one that has little relevance to the basics of the faith—has become a hill to die on, and that kind of all-or-nothing thinking prevents us from having full fellowship with each other.

But Paul made a distinction between unity in the physical realm and that in the spiritual realm. These verses in Ephesians hold out the promise that spiritual unity is not only possible but already accomplished. "Make every effort to keep the unity of the Spirit through the bond of peace," he wrote in verse 3. He told the Ephesians to "keep"—not create—unity. It was already there; he was only asking the church to maintain it.

Paul listed seven "ones"—elements that unite us as followers of Christ. Three represent the Trinity: one Spirit, one Lord, one God and Father of all. The remaining four are areas of commonality among Christians, or at least should be, according to Paul: one body, the church; one hope, the promise of eternal life; one faith, the essential doctrines of the church; and one baptism, water baptism that signifies public confession of faith. In all of these things, we have already found our unity.

One thing Paul made clear throughout his letters is that unity does not mean uniformity. He allowed and even encouraged diversity, particularly in acts of service. He also preached a fairly radical message of tolerance, given the time and place in which he was ministering. God wants you to continue to be yourself—the person he made you to be—even as you seek to promote unity in the church.

———

Lord, you want us to act in one accord as a unified body of believers, but it's so hard to imagine that coming to pass. I give you my discouragement and ask you to keep it from interfering with the small steps I can take to achieve unity with the believers in my life. I thank you that you have made us as one in the spiritual realm.

Notes

Chapter 26

1. Brennan Manning, *Reflections for Ragamuffins* (San Francisco: Harper San Francisco, 1997), p. 285.

Chapter 61

1. John MacArthur, *The MacArthur Study Bible* (Nashville: Word Publishing, 1997), p. 1021.

Chapter 64

1. Steven Curtis Chapman, Geoff Moore, "Speechless." Copyright 1999, EMI Christian Music Publishing. All rights reserved. International copyright secured.